Surrendering Oz

A Life in Essays

Surrendering Oz

A Life in Essays

BY

Bonnie Friedman

etruscan press

Etruscan Press
Wilkes University
84 West South Street
Wilkes-Barre, PA 18766
(570) 408-4546

WILKES UNIVERSITY

www.etruscanpress.org

Published 2014 by Etruscan Press
Printed in the United States of America
Cover photograph by Lisa Morrison
Cover design by Michael Ress
Interior design and typesetting by Susan Leonard
The text of this book is set in Garamond Premier Pro.

First Edition

14 15 16 17 18 5 4 3 2 1

Library of Congress Cataloguing-in-Publication Data
Friedman, Bonnie, 1958-
  Surrendering Oz : a life in essays / Bonnie Friedman. -- First edition.
    pages cm
  ISBN 978-0-9897532-2-7 (paperback)
  1. Friedman, Bonnie, 1958- 2. Women authors, American--Biography. 3. Women teachers--United States--Biography. I. Title.
  PS3606.R556Z46 2014
  814'.6--dc23
  [B]
                            2014015293

Please turn to the back of this book for a list of the sustaining funders of Etruscan Press.

TABLE OF CONTENTS

SURRENDERING OZ

A LIFE IN ESSAYS

PROLOGUE

The woman's adventure story—unlike the man's—often involves an episode of coma, a kind of prolonged death-in-life. From the moment I noticed this, as a young woman, it worried me.

In Psyche's version, which I discovered in my early thirties when I myself felt lost, the woman falls into an enchanted sleep. In Dorothy's Hollywood portrayal, the Kansas girl collapses while crossing a field of poppies. A saturating torpor descends just after the woman has won her prize—exactly when everything ought to be perfect. After all, she's achieved what the authority figure said was required. Psyche is supposed to fetch a box of underworld beauty. And she does! Dorothy possesses the witch's broom, at last! So why does their success trigger an annihilating stupor, this triumph of the unconscious, or rather, of unconsciousness?

And why, for many real women, does something similar still occur, although it's certainly no longer supposed to, not after the very real alterations that feminism's achieved? Because, despite everything, it still happens to some of us that we land the job, win the award, celebrate the marriage—and succumb to a certain bewildering joylessness, a familiar sense of fraudulence, an inability to feel the anticipated pleasure. The sensation of being insufficiently alive, of being internally even quite blotto, can afflict a woman, and a man too for that matter, for a month or a decade or an entire adulthood.

This book concerns experiences of awakening from a numb condition and springing into an enlarged awareness. It is a work of personal (often intensely personal) essays, not academic scholarship, and its focus is the disturbing, buried, radiant aspects that have been disavowed, and what happens when one repossesses them. In my own life, over and over I have struggled to accept emotional reality, tending to choose what I think ought to be true over what is true, as if I would perpetuate a soothing dream. I tend to defer anger, mourning, outsized craving, mess, whatever destabilizes, whatever demands a confrontation because in some profound way I don't want to believe confrontations are necessary.

In my actual dreams and in the events in my life that seem scripted from dreams, I have collapsed, stricken, because the central thing I need has been stolen. "Lucy Locket lost her pocket and doesn't know where to find it" is a chant that lingers from childhood. My mother read it to me from a favorite library book. How could you lose your pocket, I wondered. It sounded like losing your soul. And what to make of the correspondence between the heroine's name, which links her very identity to possession of an internal, hidden compartment (for wasn't a locket a type of pocket?) and the loss of that essential part? And, if the girl doesn't have it from the outset, can it ever be restored?

I recalled Lucy Locket years later when venturing off to see a psychotherapist—something I did often in my early thirties, trying this expert and then that in a string of offices across Manhattan, some of them perched atop midtown towers, others in brownstone basement hideaways, and still others in those chambers buried in the megaliths of the Upper West Side, hushed twilight consulting rooms whose limestone portals flank the side streets of the apartment blocks, normal-size doors set within towering mortised frames—like entering the side of the Sphinx itself. In each case

I approached the therapist's office feeling both hopeful and ill. I yearned to be cured of my unhappiness but clutched within myself a certain truth I couldn't bear to have validated, or rather, a truth I didn't want to be told was significant, essential.

I was terrified to hear that my clumsy, coarse unhappiness actually mattered, perverse as that sounds. At the time, my life with my husband was going through a malaise; I didn't feel he was attracted to me, and it seemed to me that all around the city stood women and men necking in doorways, women and men in evening outfits waiting on line to go dancing, to drink, to kiss, while I myself felt sealed shut, exempted, somehow increasingly virginal.

But sex was simply just the most nameable part of what seemed wrong. Things within me had become off-kilter, increasingly loosely connected, even frankly oblique, as if I were a rattletrap jalopy that needed to have its bolts tightened, or as if I'd missed a crucial life lesson that everyone now took so entirely for granted they couldn't even articulate it; they had incorporated it. Still, might I be cured without having to discomfit those with whom I lived—my husband, and, at a greater distance, my parents, not to mention my own self? Could I be fixed, that is, *secretly*? I desperately wanted to feel better—the sense of meaning had dropped out of my life; I felt there was nothing really to look forward to—while at the same time I did not want to believe that the actual felt experience of my life ought to be of crucial significance, even to me.

After these therapy sessions, which felt like bacchanalias of self-revelation, I staggered up the blazing sidewalk unable to make full use of what I'd heard from the therapist. Fragments of her responses swirled in the air. And so I set her words into notebooks. I believed that the notebooks would make what the therapist had said feel more real—the statements would resonate ever more loudly between cardboard covers—while also saving up the insights for the future time when I might afford to act. That is, the notebook both reinforced what the therapist had said and, at the same time, buried its power. It was real-making and denaturing, at once.

One notebook gave way to another. Soon I had a shelf of them. I had a wall. The notebooks received my revelations with endless nonjudgmental attention and so I remained ignorant while they grew wise. I could rarely bear to open them, although occasionally, when moving from one home to the next, I found myself turning the pages of a crackling yellow-paged volume. A gust of delirium pixilated me, while at the same time my head grew heavy and I longed to sleep. The notebooks reminded me of all I had left unfinished and aroused a sense that life was passing me by.

But then my life took a turn. I accepted a job, my first real grown-up job although I had entered my forties, and I was flung out into a demanding world of classrooms—for I was a professor now—in which it was imperative that I allowed myself to know what I knew both about literature (which I had been studying passionately for decades) and about the internal world of feeling-states (essential to understanding the nuance of stories). I had to trust my instincts and make use of gut knowledge, whereas before I'd been cerebral, cautious, and sequestered—passing much of my life in the tiny, shadowy, silent room at the rear of our apartment.

I was visible every day now, and although in the beginning the person in the classrooms felt fraudulent—how she craved approval, at the outset!—more and more of the time she seemed true, she seemed me. My voice slowed and even lowered somewhat. I took my time. I breathed more deeply. I felt increasingly real, and alive. I challenged my husband when it felt asphyxiatingly urgent that I do so—before this, little about my emotions seemed urgent; all was infinitely malleable—and, over time, I discovered how to advocate for myself with less drama and more grace. It was not such a big deal! I just said what I thought, without having to first get all worked up about it.

I hadn't known that this was part of the problem between us—a certain reticence. My husband, taking my cue (or perhaps he'd been this way all along), seemed to welcome this new direct-ness. I caught him looking at me in a new way. Things were simple, not so thickety and wrought as before. "Stay in your body when I hug you!" I told him, for I realized that he seemed to evanesce, as if he'd become an empty suit of armor. He had his reasons for distancing himself and I heard them, and it was the beginning of the journey back for both of us. What I had been looking for had arrived in this boomerang way.

Lucy Locket lost her pocket—she flung open the clasp of her-self only to see a flat absence. She was a person who called out but heard no echo. She looked out and didn't see, on others' faces, a response to her own. That had been my own childhood truth, of course. My own mother had been depressed. She said I was "too much," and I believed I was. Too loud, too energetic, too needy, too stupid, too intense. She wanted to sit in silence and read a magazine, turning the varnished knife-blue pages of *McCall's*, feast-ing on the happy families since her own original family had left her bereft. I sat beside her on the linoleum and quietly turned the wood blocks of alphabet letters, astonished at how a *W* became the jagged empty slots of a twin canoe, and an *I* the beam on which an entire house could rest.

My mother's ankleted foot beside me, the air hissing from the radiator steam, I built the wood blocks into towers, holding my breath, as if, if I were quiet enough, the god of physical reality would grant me a special dispensation and allow my efforts to end in success rather than failure. I might erect a column to the very ceiling! One winter morning I sat so rigid and breathless that my pulse jumped in my cheekbones, and a seventh letter allowed itself to rest on the bending wood tower of the other six. Oh, my gosh, yes. I'd never arrived at seven.

My hand poised an eighth on top and I held it, my chest thudding. My eyeballs itched from staring, but I was afraid to blink. Then, molecule by sticky molecule, I gradually opened forefinger and thumb. The tower held. The blocks stood glued together by some triumphant, kind divinity—oh, the beauty that I'd been granted to see!—and then, as I watched, utterly motionless, all came slamming down with a clattering crash. My mother did not look up. She was in her own hard-won, separate world. I fetched the letters back and began again.

As I grew, the kingdom of letters increased its thrall. Afternoons during grade school I sat with a book on a sky-blue wood chair in front of my Bronx apartment building. My favorite volume, printed on glazed leaves and far heavier than it looked, shone inky letters up at me, each one the color of Superman's hair. It told biblical stories of majestic beauty. The letters themselves composed a dark palace, and sometimes I read the stories and sometimes merely gazed at the tiny, glistening blue-black mirrors reflecting the shimmer of the world behind my shoulders, each flickering ghost suggesting a reality I couldn't discern directly.

And thus, like my mother, I began to enter my own hard-won separate world, in a culture where women were still encouraged to remain locked inside a dream. It wasn't until many years later, in classrooms where I welcomed the lost and wandering aspects of my own students and then ultimately of myself, that I was able to feel coherent. What I had inside me, what my students had inside them, was both valid and crucial, I finally could believe.

Psyche must journey into the underworld to win back the treasure she lacks. The underworld of the ancients is not, I discovered, Hell. It is, instead, the land of shades where our ancestors

exist after their days are spent, and it is a repository of wisdom—
Hades being a god of wealth as well as death. It is to this place that
Psyche must descend. And so the woman whose name means "soul,"
frightened, alone, summons her courage. She is on a quest to get
a container of beauty. Sacred beauty! Beauty from a goddess. The
queen sets a box of it in her hands.

On her journey back, how can Psyche not peek inside? Who
wouldn't want to know the secret? Yet the box marked "beauty"
actually contains sleep, and so the heroine stumbles, tumbles, lies
comatose. "Poppies!" the Wicked Witch had crooned, swirling her
wand, setting her trap. And, racing merrily across that brilliant red
field, Dorothy gradually slows, and then comes to a stop, wavering,
limbs drunk with languor. She yawns. A blissful smile stretches
across her face. Asleep, the young woman can dwell in Oz forever.
Asleep, she need never liberate the poor mortal behind the curtain
from his own servitude as the wizard, she need never confront the
reality that the fantasy must end. Down she sinks, and nestles her
head in the scarlet blossoms. Her friends cannot break the thrall.

What does? The gift of the immaculate white witch: pricks
of stinging snow. Icy truth, brisk logic—these are the traits that
open Dorothy's eyes, at last. Here is adulthood. Here is the force
of bracing reality. The heroine hoists herself out of her delirium
and sets off on the last stage of her journey. She must surrender
toxic fantasy so that she can at last handle potent, gritty, black-and-
white-spectrum reality, with all of its limitations and powers. She
must surrender the Oz of dreamland stupor in order to become
the master of her own life.

We thought what was in the box was beauty but it was sleep.
We thought it was perfection but it was a trance. Where is your
anger, friends routinely ask. Why aren't you angry at your mother
for how she treated you as a child? And why aren't you angry at me
when I don't do what I say I will, a particular childhood girlfriend

XVI | BONNIE FRIEDMAN

inquires. I just am not. Instead, I'm enraged at the dog that barks in the neighbor's yard and the leaf blower that bellows for an hour at a stretch, and the universe itself that has conspired to steal from me my voice—which I had believed was something until I convinced myself it was nothing.

To gain their independence, boys must steal the key hidden under their mother's pillow, according to Robert Bly. And girls? He doesn't say. Our key, I think, is not hidden under the mother's pillow. It is hidden in the voice of the barking dog, in the smug, envied ogre who sashays about, in our irritation at the day itself for having so few useful hours in it, in the antique but nevertheless commanding conviction that our needs are ugly and excessive, in the exquisite trances we still inhabit.

Although—wait. Come to think of it, the frozen drowse *did* contain an eerie beauty. There Psyche lies in a ditch. Her estranged husband, Eros, comes upon her, and, surprised into pity, touches her with the tip of his arrow—echoing the way she wounded him earlier, while he slept, with a scald of candle wax. Awakened, she is granted eternal life for the risks she undertook, and indeed she remains alive today in her famous story. Underworld beauty was both the occasion for the stupor and ultimately its cure. Taboo knowledge, fetched from the depths, resists being brought into ordinary consciousness and yet is the cure for the dissociative dream state.

The essays in this book all have to do with encountering an underworld beauty, an estranged, buried, yet magical and long-missed, unintegrated aspect of oneself. My own life story has been a series of expansions and expansions, and then almost stunned languors, marvelous times of discovery followed by comatose episodes that summoned the next stage of growth. Sometimes I had to learn the same lesson twice, the second time at a more elemental level.

And often I was staring in one direction only to discover that my salvation came from another quadrant entirely. Luckily, a fresh, strange guide always eventually appeared, answering a call I didn't even know I was making, stepping out of some realm of experience about which I'd previously been blind.

These essays do two things. They examine telling aspects of my own story and they tacitly reflect on themes in women's lives today. They are all about yearning for the missing element. One writes to discover how one has gotten lost, and to forge out of language a magic key. Often the key to one locked soul turns out to be the key to another, for we are not so different. Beneath the disguise of our faces are common conflicts, common struggles. Perhaps you, the reader, will find in these essays some keys to your own lost zones, and a way to be roused from your own transfixed dream states, the particular stuck places on your own journey.

Coming of Age in Book Country

I knew I was back in New York when I saw children walking to
school with books open in their hands. I'd lived away for fifteen years. Now down the streets of Brooklyn they drifted, novels
spread wide between their palms, the actual world comprising a
mere running margin of asphalt and high-heeled shoes and honk-
ing cars. The massive knapsacks sagging off their backs seemed a
wise precaution against the danger of the children floating right
off into the realms of imagination that lured them down the street
transfixed, one foot set absently in front of the next.

I'd been the same way not long ago. Growing up in the Bronx,
I read myself to P.S. 24 in the morning and read myself home each
afternoon. My best friends were fanatical readers—Emily, a science
wizard who used wads of pink Kleenex for bookmarks, and Stacy,
who, despite our apartment life, penned guides on the best way to
lay out an herb garden and how to ride horses in proper English
style, ramrod straight, a moss-velvet riding helmet on one's head.
She read me her work leaning against the cyclone fence in the J.H.S.
141 school yard near the kids slamming handballs.

It seemed perfectly natural to us that our parents owned
novels set in our own city—*The Chosen, A Tree Grows in Brooklyn,
Where Are You Going? Out. What Are You Doing? Nothing*, and a
bevy of Mafia tales. Even then we sensed that the city was always

1

being reinvented and pulped. The streets were jackhammered constantly; we looked for squares of fresh cement in which to finger our names. New York was book country because it was half real and half imagined, as were we ourselves. Hadn't a storybook boy spent the night at the Metropolitan Museum? Didn't my brother tell me about a young man in a novel who worried about the ducks in Central Park—where did they go in the winter? After that, I worried about them too.

Every book was a book of spells, and we longed to transform ourselves. My friends and I were like James Gatz, yearning to climb up the moonlight ladder to where blond gods quaff nectar in spangled rooms. How tired we were of long division and ink splotches, of tedious pretests and retests, and of being chosen almost last in gym games. The girls chosen first read *Seventeen*, not *The Island of the Blue Dolphins*. And they smelled of Herbal Essence, not the stone halls of the Cloisters, where we drifted about in states of mystical transport on Sunday afternoons.

We longed for adventure, and the revelation of one's true inner identity, which had nothing to do with the face in the mirror or popularity or grades, but with the crown tips of letters themselves and the perpetual twilight in the original old-growth forest maintained deep in the Botanical Gardens—leaf-mold scent drifting up, shadow doorways appearing and vanishing.

My friends and I passed around *Act One* by Moss Hart, a Bronx boy who ended up living at the Waldorf. His wife, Kitty Carlisle, on *To Tell the Truth*, always clasped an invisible martini in her hand. You'd never have known she'd been raised Cohen. My friend Stacy's father brought us all to the Tiki Room at the Plaza for her eleventh birthday, and we ate with chopsticks and sipped virgin pineapple blender drinks, and the reek of the Bunsen burners was the most sophisticated scent I'd ever inhaled.

The other patrons glowered. We were a table of shrieky girls. I longed to be a grown-up with a long white cashmere dress like the woman across the room, for a man to notice me through the candlelight. And yet the theatricality of the marble-corridored hotel made me consider the presence of its invisible author—the person who put the waiters in tuxes and who arranged the palms in the Palm Court, where a storybook girl ate lunch. Even then it seemed clear that Manhattan was composed and calculated, like a wildly concocted plot, but that I would get to play a part in it merely by maturing, as if the city were something I would grow into like a shoe.

Every other issue of *New York* magazine in those days—the early seventies—carried, it seemed, a cover story about a house-wife with a secret life. This one hung out with drug addicts. This one posed for girlie pix. It seemed clear that to live in New York was to have a secret life, and it was only a matter of getting older and finding out what yours would be. Who needed the unconscious? New York was the unconscious. Waiting for my friend Emily outside Hunter Junior High, I asked a man, "Do you have the time?" "If you've got the place," he answered. I swiv-eled my head away and let my eyes follow a city bus, as though I didn't understand.

But I knew what his words meant, and was flattered and frightened. And what if I'd said, "I don't have the place, but do you?" What would happen then? If you could dream it, it could happen in New York—that seemed keenly true to me at thirteen. My friends and I carried our secret lives before us like emblems, and read them as we walked to school, and read them on the bus. The city itself was a library of apartment buildings, each with stories spooling down echoey corridors and with dialogue leaking through the plasterboard. Often we put a cup to the wall so we could hear it better. "Shhh!" we'd say to our families, glaring, fingers to our lips, ears shoved hard against the glass.

My friends and I read only novels. Nonfiction did not exist, despite Stacy's pamphlets on how to live the cultivated British life. It wasn't until late in junior high, when a friend showed me a book outlining the five ballet positions, that I considered the possibility that volumes stuffed with facts might actually be real books. But what sad books they seemed! How thin—no matter their sprawl and heft. Books of fact all seemed like math, as if a thousand wood pointers were banging against a thousand chalkboards on which were inscribed life's rock-hard realities. How frightening! I was terrible at school. I was in fact terrible at everything except reading, which at the time seemed about as useful as whittling.

Years later—my first job out of college—I found myself working on a definitive book of facts, *The Guinness Book of World Records*. The country of books had sucked me up for good. I sat beside the proofreader on the twenty-sixth floor of a deco sky-scraper and read copy aloud to him. The man with the longest fingernails, which twirled from his fingertips like paper party noisemakers. The man who'd drifted the longest time at sea. The Siamese twins scissoring away from each other, dapper, married to sisters. Out the office window the sunset laid siege to New Jersey. It hovered from three p.m. on in shades of hibiscus and tangerine. I didn't want to hear it was pollution, something the production manager felt obliged to explain. I was so happy to have a job in Manhattan involving books.

The proofreader and I ate dried pineapple chunks and cashews from brown paper sleeves we'd bought at lunch. He told me that I resembled a young Leslie Caron. I was obscurely attracted to him, and went over to his apartment on West Ninety-Fourth, and watched a sea of glittering cockroaches recede miraculously into the walls, and then sat on his mattress on the floor and gazed at Fred Astaire dancing with Ginger Rogers through a TV screen thick with haze. Women's faces peered down from the apartment walls, dozens of them ripped from magazines and taped three feet from the floor: Bette Davis, Jean Harlow, all seeming to smolder with disapproval, as if his superego were female, as if he would feel its eyes on him even in the dark.

"I'll never make a play for you," said the proofreader to me at a Beefsteak Charlie's on Thirty-Fourth Street. "Don't expect that I will."

But I was still so averse to facts I had no idea what he meant. The next time I came over he showed me his feather collection— bluebird feathers, wild turkey feathers, and many feathers of unknown origin, tawny, with a triangular eye at the top as if an inky pen had been allowed to bleed. He kept them crammed in a brown paper lunch bag in his closet, so many that the sides of the bag were round. For how long had he been collecting them? "Draw the feather across your upper lip," he instructed. "Doesn't it feel nice?" "Oh, it does," I answered. Then he walked me to the subway. An enormous sadness seemed to fill the night. I thought wildly: "I should stay with him until he's happy!" I thought this mad thought even as he waved to me from the top of the stairs. How I would have liked to dash up to him! How I would have liked to touch the bearded texture of his cheek!

His grandfather had been an illustrious publisher: the first to publish James Joyce in the United States. This heritage weighed heavily on the proofreader, who disbelieved himself worthy of it. The proofreader himself was easier to talk to than almost any man I'd ever met. He carried a Channel 13 tote with orange print on canvas, and took me to see *Casablanca* at the Thalia, and he told me about New Orleans, where he'd grown up fatherless, but always this wild melancholy seemed to throb around us, and it glued me to him. I kept thinking that if I could just get closer or stay longer, the melancholy would disperse.

One day, the proofreader was fired. He'd been proofing fewer and fewer galley pages. When he averaged less than two a day, he was dismissed. Meanwhile I'd been promoted to editing children's joke books and puzzle books. Soon I departed for Boston, which was cheaper and where I thought I might at last learn to write. A decade later, visiting my parents, I saw the proofreader on the platform at Forty-Second Street, about to board the #1 uptown. "Oh!" I gasped, but didn't exert myself to call his name.

He looked so familiar I had the ridiculous feeling that I'd be seeing him again soon anyway, which of course I never did. But our strange romance—watching dance movies, reading aloud the jerky and now antiquated language of proofing (*caps, ques, bang*), and the strong scent of Mitchum aftershave contained in his bathroom—all returned to me.

How long I had remained in ignorance!—even after he told me about a very close male friend of his who liked to dress up in stockings and brassiere. Even after he told me that he'd never had a girlfriend in his adulthood. He had announced himself to me as explicitly as he could bear but I maintained my perverse innocence, and felt forever that we were on the edge of a breakthrough of intimacy that would somehow resolve our mutual melancholy. I refused to read his secret life, which he had come to New York to live.

My own got resolved through the mirrored halls of sentences. I found myself in prose. And he, I suspect, discovered himself in the meeting places of the city. He phoned me once, a few months after he was fired. "I've called to tell you something," he said. "I've joined a weekly group for people like me. I can't elaborate. But I'm much happier now." Even then—it was 1981—I had no idea what he meant. I simply refused to believe, of course, what I already knew, which was that the erotic haze around us would always remain as unconsummatable as the romance of a reader for a character in a book.

After I hung up I stood there with my hand on my parents' mustard-colored phone, pondering what he meant by "weekly group for people like me." My mother glanced up from her *Short Story International.* The #100 bus hauled by, up 239th Street. Both my ignorance and my insight came from bookishness, I knew. How much bigger my life might be if I could thrust aside my books! And yet I couldn't really picture a life bigger than a life in books. I'd grown up in book country and it was where I meant to live. I picked up "Hills Like White Elephants," which I happened to be reading even though I had no idea what it was about. What did it mean, for the woman to have an operation to "let the air in"? And why were the man and the woman in the story in such bad moods? I needed to read everything much more closely, I suddenly felt with an urgency that made my head pound. I could scarcely bear the weight of my own ignorance. Try to understand, try to understand, I told myself, bending over the book again. Why was I so obtuse?

I stared at the type so closely that it seemed a pillared temple-front colonnade I could enter. The mattress creaked in my father's bedroom as he turned, drowsing, taking a break from his worries. My mother flipped a page of her magazine. The world around me was bewildering, unkempt, shifting, repetitive, and with no index or glossary, no chapter titles. But although there was much I didn't understand in my reading, there was much that I did. I recognized the girl saying fanciful, clever things—performing. And the longing of the young man to stay at the bar where the people are "reasonable." "What is your group?" I wanted to ask the proofreader. "How are you happier? Why are you calling me?" Afraid to demand the answers of life, I bent closer to the page. The city itself waited patiently, constructing and destroying and raising itself again at the end of the subway line. Sitting at my way station, I realized that an era of my life had ended. It was possible to change one's fate; one could be happier. How? The book told me the answer but I was not yet willing to pay the price it stipulated and so kept on reading, although I was sick at heart.

How I Learned to Think

In the years before I discovered how to think, I was lucky enough to have two best friends. They lived in opposite directions, and every day at three p.m. outside J.H.S. 141 in the Bronx we stood on a corner and they sang to me, "Walk my way." "No, walk my way." I always chose to walk with Stacy, who was mean, rather than Emily, who was understanding. Still, I would toss imploring looks over my shoulder at Emily as I vanished down the street as if to say, "I adore you, you can see I'm helpless, can't you? Stacy's an ogre, I have no choice in this, and you are my absolute favorite."

And Emily was. She was a passionate, windswept, science-besotted only child always in the grips of a cold, and with hot-pink crumpled tissues tumbling out the sleeves of her sweaters, and innumerable missed days at school. Our emblem was Nostradamus's prophesying, severed head lurching across a laboratory floor—we'd seen it on *Creature Feature* one Friday night when the rest of the world was asleep. First we'd turned off the bedroom lights and held aloft lit wands of sparklers—a seething fountain of stars and asterisks scorching into our gaze an instant before they wove into the air our names, and then, after a further spewing, blinding moment, divined the names of our husbands, the cities we'd visit, the artistic or scientific works we'd accomplish, the lolloping, incandescent skirts we'd wear someday, before the guttering nub scorched our fingertips. (Emily's father had brought home the illegal silver stalks from New Jersey; her parents were divorced and he

9

was always corrupting her with treats, for which she held him in resolute contempt.) After that, we'd eaten string cheese we frayed with our fingers, a sophisticated delectable "gourmet food," a braid of caraway seeds and tangy fat, and watched, glaze eyed, from our beds, as across the rough-hewn Gothic lair came Nostradamus's chopped-off head, still alive, jolting forward on its stump of neck, ranting its visions of the future.

"Nostradamus's head!" we murmured to each other after that, and burst out laughing to ward off our horror of that unvanquished skull. In those days it was unknown what would become of us. Women intellectuals still had something of the mutant and pitiful about them: Madame Curie sickened by her radium, "She's in the library!" a howl of horror rising out of *It's a Wonderful Life*. Emily and I were bookish girls—she even more than I because she could indulge her passions, having no siblings and a bedroom of her own in which to pile her ever-increasing volumes.

She stayed up however late she pleased. As long as she was physically in bed by ten p.m., her mother didn't monitor. The door to her room was solid oak. Emily read novels to her heart's content under her black-light blanket. At last, losing the train of the story, she turned off the overhead and flicked a switch on a midnight bulb, and her blanket pulsed with phosphorescent hot-pink lines, whorls and carbuncles and exploded fingerprints, the insignia of the maze of existence itself somehow, a labyrinth burning the dark.

No such decoration in my own bedroom, which I shared with my sister. I taped up only the earth from space, a circle isolated far off in a sea of black; it had been given away at school. Anything else was mockable—likely to inspire my older siblings' ridicule. I played no records of my own, hung no art of my own, certainly lit no incense of my own, all of which Emily did without a second thought. It was as if, instead of my being merely a Bronx daughter of a newly middle-class family, I were some orphan ward, beholden.

I returned to Emily, still sealed, the album of *Hair* she'd given me as a birthday gift, with its acid green and sickly lemon color-fields clashing behind a young man's backlit, luminous 'fro. We played Emily's copy of that record over and over in her bedroom—"LBJ, IRT, USA, LSD," the chorus dreamily harmonized—but my family's stereo sat in our living room. I couldn't possibly enjoy listening to those songs in my own house! Wasn't that obvious to Emily?

And yet I craved what seemed her daring verve. We both fell in love with Tony Curtis in *The Great Race*, but she bought a chunky, toppling paperback that listed every picture he was in, and she spent her final year of junior high watching each and every one, even if it came on at three thirty or four a.m. She cranked her round neon-orange wind-up alarm that exploded with a firehouse jangle, and then set a checkmark beside each movie once it was seen. In contrast, my own passion remained flat, static, hidden within me like a wick engulfed in paraffin. She and I both prized self-forgetfulness but only she pursued it. And I found that aggravatingly admirable—that she did the thing, she did it, whatever anyone might think!

Whereas Stacy, in contrast, was worldly. She never dismissed what others might think. By "success" she meant precisely what most people meant. She was an impeccably groomed, ambitious, pragmatic figure sweeping down the street in a long coat that gave her the silhouette of a queen on a chess set. I was drawn to her because she too was a girl of imagination, a girl ablaze, although her focus was altogether different. She folded and stapled pretend bankbooks and induced me to invest my allowance dollars with her, and she took lessons riding English-style on horses in Harrison, New York, her hips hoisted aloft as the horse loped, her spine straight as our teacher's wooden pointer. Her father was a corporate lawyer, and it was assumed that she, being the eldest, and clever, would triumph in life as well. He drove a low white Jag like the runabout on the Monopoly set, and they summered on Fire Island, where she wore low-slung bellbottoms streaked with bleach, and her mother shopped for clothes only at "boutiques."

"Are skinny-legged jeans in, in Riverdale?" Stacy asked the last time we spoke. She'd finally moved to Harrison after years of riding lessons there, and now owned a horse, and planted an herb garden, and had a live-in maid. "A live-in maid, Bonnie!" she repeated when my response was insufficient. Her father had even made a postcard of their sumptuous Tudor house, which she'd shown me the last time I visited. The postcard was 1950s sepia-toned, with a scalloped edge—a campy artifact whose jolly façade and cool irony impressed me. And then she called with her question. She had a new set of girlfriends whom I heard laughing in the background. "I can't stay on," she declared. But, well, Harrison was ahead of Riverdale fashionwise, wasn't it, she seemed curious to establish—by phoning me, her last contact in that old outpost, someone oblivious to the looks of things.

"Skinny-legged jeans?" I asked, racking my brain. "No, I don't think I've seen anything like that."

"I thought not," said Stacy and hung up.

I hung up too, a moment later. Skinny-legged jeans. Obviously they were trivial—being mere fashion—and yet if they were completely trivial, then why were my cheeks blazing, why did my throat and chest sting?

I was lost within myself and remained so for a decade, unable to draw conclusions about anything, living as if my mind were a door I must hold open for yet more information, as if, if I came to a conclusion too soon, I would miss the crucial valence of things, the particular nuance that provided the key. Only when I had sufficient information could I determine what things meant.

In the meantime I sat for hours behind a curtain swept around my semicircular chair, a book open in my hands as my brothers and sister rampaged through the house. My parents had a multivolume set of Dickens, the type crimped into the binding so that the lines of text ascended, a rising mountainside I climbed, happiest when I'd disappeared entirely into a story. The more demanding the act of reading, the more thoroughly I disappeared. Even the heavy stamp of the print into the pulpy yellow paper made me happy, as if each letter were a sunken compartment in which I might hide.

"Bon-don-lonchikle!" my brothers often crooned to me, a name derived from some creepy old man on a public bench who had moaned that while pinching my cheeks. "Bon-don-lonchikle!" they laughed, but the strung-out moniker seemed to capture a truth: it identified my secret self, spazzy, twitchy, a *girl*! For in those days, the word that named my gender often curled like a lubricious smirk. "Here, girly!" said the pimply man who sold pizza slices for twenty-five cents. "Take it, girly," said the man who offered six-cent candy. Something mortifying was all over me, something that inspired lewdness and condescension. And this something helped to explain, I believed, why I was stupid, carrying home barely passable grades from school on the Friday retest, having no idea of how to use the mind I possessed. How did the other children know the answers?

I believed that some of them—the most brilliant ones—managed to pick up the right answers from the general atmosphere of the schoolroom and that others came with the information somehow ambiently preinstalled from their homes, knowledge drifting in from the sea of conversation in which they'd grown. But even when a teacher called me to the blackboard and explained the lesson, I was like a stunned cat. I stared and swallowed, distracted by the glare of the teacher's attention, the loudspeaker roar of her voice.

Released, I raced back to my chair, content to be stupid as long as I could be ignored. I truly believed I was mostly invisible, and passed my days with a novel held open under my desk, obliviously offering my teacher the wandering part in my uncombed hair. The bright boys, my classmates, plump children in button-down shirts so white they were blue, played the violin with a handkerchief pressed fussily under their downtucked chin like Haifetz and rallied their facts like a lieutenant. Some even flirted with me, but I found it merely mortifying. "Don't look at me. Don't notice!"

I was in a state of being uninvented, unseen, private. I didn't know how to value my own observations. Sochial Studies, I wrote on my loose-leaf tab. When a boy sitting near me laughed at my spelling, I laughed, too. My pages tore at their unreinforced holes and their top right corners hatcheted down. As the months progressed I obliviously added more and more paper to the binder until the crammed wedge of pages balked when I tried to move from one tabbed subject to another. Almost instantly infuriated, I grabbed a recalcitrant heap and mauled it over the rings. The teeth of the binder sprang open, jagged, and out leapt a passel of pages to splay across the floor. I didn't respect my own work. Why should I? I didn't know that respecting one's work was a trait that could be cultivated, and that respect actually often precedes achievement.

At the start of ninth grade it was announced that in October the tests would be administered for New York City's specialized high schools. My father grimly said he would help me study for the Bronx Science exam. Both of my brothers were attending Science, and it was assumed that this would launch their futures (as indeed it did: one went into medicine, the other became an engineer at MIT Research Corporation)—but they were far more grounded in the world than I. They took apart toasters and assembled them again; they understood about vacuum tubes and electrical currents, and even laser beams. Nevertheless, on Saturday mornings I sat with my supplies—a battery of sharpened goldenrod Ticonderoga #2 pencils (specified by my father) and a kitchen timer that muttered "tsk, tsk, tsk,"—and worked my way through the mock exam.

Occasionally I employed a desiccated eraser hard as a Jujube, leaving a shaming dark smudge. Once I didn't use a #2, and my father, infuriated at the faintness of my handwriting (and, I suppose, my ill-disciplined, lassitudinous mind), grew red in the face and, yelling, snatched up that wrong pencil and threw it hard into the empty tin trash can, where it exploded like a cherry bomb. Other times he merely sighed, shoving his hand against his forehead. I was hopeless—and as surprised as anyone when Bronx Science accepted me.

I explained this to myself by recalling that, when I'd written my address on the index card that the proctor distributed, I'd printed the x in Bronx in a special way. My left-to-right stroke curved like a sine wave while the right-to-left stroke was strictly straight. This was how scientists inscribed the letter, my brothers had instructed me. An influential person must have noticed the secret insignia. Rationally I understood that there was likely more to my acceptance than this, but in the back of my mind I still saw that x.

The first day of high school it thrilled me to step through the doors of the school under the famous lofting Venetian glass mosaic (legend had it that the school had bought this rather than a swimming pool), and in fact over the years to come I never failed to enter without at least flinging a respectful glance up at Archimedes with his splayed compass taking the measure of the world, Charles Darwin dressed in street clothes of brown serge, and Madame Curie with her glittering test tube, charting the radiant realms. Madame Curie! There she towered dozens of feet tall, discovering an incandescent element that emitted gamma rays (I'd read a biography of her in sixth grade), and that occurred in minute quantities in the alchemical-sounding mineral pitchblende. Her notebooks were so radioactive they were stored in boxes lined with lead. Beneath these Olympians twinkled the words EVERY GREAT ADVANCE IN SCIENCE HAS ISSUED FROM A NEW

AUDACITY OF IMAGINATION—JOHN DEWEY. Impressive phrases, and it required a humanist to write them! I walked in under that banner of poetry, not at all sure I belonged there, as at Bronx Science I still got terrible grades, but heartened by the shimmering vision nonetheless.

And then, one day in my second year, my American history teacher, Mr. Harrison, explained how to study, and my brain began to perform. Halleluyah! Facts stuck to it! I loved to practice this teacher's method, which was to read through the textbook chapter while my hand scribbled notes, then to shut the book and set down all I'd retained. Apparently the path to my head was through my hand, for I swiftly recalled more and more, as if I were stocking the shelves of my mind. I did thrillingly well on tests, for the first time in my life. 98s. 97s. The glittering apex of the grading system. I cinched my belt tighter, having discovered anorexia at the same time, and walked home merrily from Bronx Science under the roaring elevated train. Perhaps I wasn't worthless after all.

As my brain developed, my body dwindled. In junior high I'd obliviously plumped up on A&P jellyrolls and deep-fried knishes and French toast with maple syrup—treats I allowed myself right after school. One day when I was in high school, though, my mother beckoned me to look into the mirror, and suddenly I had a body, and it was one with knobby hips and a gaping shirt. I associated this pudgy body with my stupidity, and began to carve away at both. Each Monday evening I sat beside my mother on a metal folding chair at the local Y and listened to the Weight Watchers lecturer, a kind man with loopy hair and expansive gestures, and then I carried home with me a fresh blank food chart on which to write down all I ate.

I loved filling out the chart. I loved noticing what before had been invisible. I seemed to be extracting myself out of oblivion. And I loved best of all when, at the start of each meeting on

Monday, I stood in my stocking feet on the scale and the lecturer nudged the wedge of iron along the bar to establish my new weight. 104. 103 and a half. I was presented a black round pin holding a diamond sliver that glinted like a drop of Curie's radium. I grew so thin that a new hole needed to be gouged in my belt, and then another new hole. I was happier than I'd ever believed I could be. I'd found a power. I'd discovered I could influence my life.

Still, I didn't confuse the high grades I got at school with actual thought. It was merely performing a good trick, like playing three-dimensional tic-tac-toe. Still, my grades got me accepted into a liberal arts college that had a library reference room lined with faded tapestries. Every night from six p.m. until midnight I sat in one of the creaky, black-painted Windsor chairs and read the assigned books, underlining, copying out, savoring the monastic existence, which felt like virtue incarnate. I sipped scalding coffee with chalky whitener dispensed from a machine in the basement, and, on study breaks ate so many carrots my skin tinged orange.

Then, junior year of college I fell in love with a droll senior, and the anorexia ended. I gave up the charts on which I wrote down everything that I ate. Happiness itself was a bleary drug. For lunch I bought kaiser rolls and fresh sliced provolone cheese at a corner deli and picnicked with my boyfriend on his bed. When I was awarded Phi Beta Kappa I learned the fraternity handshake but didn't invite my parents to the initiation. I believed that secretly I was still that girl unable properly to add things up because I hadn't yet kicked shut that door inside me. It was still hanging wide. I was awaiting the signal that I had taken in sufficient information to be allowed to come to my own conclusions, to be a separate person.

In the meantime I remained merged somehow with those around me, agreeable, compliant. I understood that my perspective was often distorted, and that such a person should not draw conclusions. It was as if I had one giant eye and one tiny one, one eye the size of a jar lid and the other the size of a sewing needle's. I responded with too much enthusiastic intensity to some situations, and at other times missed the crucial ramification and responded with a mechanical, irresponsible nonchalance. At some point in the future when my eyes were the same size, which would happen because I'd taken in sufficient information and had acquired some kind of balance, *then* I would trust myself to form judgments. I was waiting to have sufficient information to warrant being allowed to come to conclusions. When was enough information enough?

"There's a garbage-y smell in here," announced a friend in graduate school, stepping into my apartment for a party.

Only in retrospect did that rankle. Why not take me aside to tell me that, I wondered the next morning. At the time I merely blushed hard, and ran out of my party with the trash.

I was, in my life, in a kind of coma. I believed, as many girls do, that the signals that came from inside were frivolous, half mad, silly, arbitrary, a blinding, burning fountain signifying nothing. I was estranged from myself, a kind of split-off Nostradamus head lurching my way forward in life without benefit of internal, and often bodily, signals. And then I was asked to teach. I was a second-year student at the Iowa Writers' Workshop, and assigned a literature class. It was late August, sweltering.

I stood before my first-ever session in the turquoise scratchy polyester frilled dress in which I'd attended my sister's wedding. A pockmarked, smirking boy in the furthest row tilted back on the hind legs of his chair and clicked his pen. A girl in the first row with blonde, shellacked orange-juice-can curls peered at me, a blank notebook open on her desk. I was teaching *Macbeth*. I'd reread *Macbeth*.

"Macbeth is a man at war with his own conscience," I suddenly announced to my students, and to myself. "There's no feeling safe, for him!" Not knowing how to teach, I had anxiously abandoned my notes and begun to lecture, to conjure. Knives floating in the air, bloody hands that choke the throat of their own mistress, a ghost sitting silently at a party, a voice announcing, "Macbeth hath murdered sleep!"—"Why, this was just the Bronx!" I exclaimed, glimpsing it now for the first time. It was where I'd grown up. It was people disclaiming the meaning of their actions, constantly. It was the language of your inner reality divorced from what you were willing to acknowledge.

I recalled my sister pinching my cheeks so hard between pincerlike fingers that my skin throbbed for half an hour afterwards, even as she smiled the whole time in my face and I convinced myself this was love. And my mother fretting over Anita's fleshiness with a fascinated concern that seemed to have a knife blade hidden inside it.

Shakespeare's play was all about the disparity between the felt truth and the one publicly enacted, I heard my own voice say. It was the refused truth of things exploded outward. It was self-estrangement enacted on the world. It was another way of being a doofus. Of course the witches offered temptations! The world will do that. It will offer lots of glimmering rewards if only you will ignore what you know is true.

The boy clicked his pen, but less. The girl had taken a note or two, nodding slowly.

Walking uphill on Jefferson Street after class, I thought: So, in teaching literature, how you register the emotional valences matters. You can't afford to be comatose. The institution—the university—*values* the felt sense of things! Has to! There's no teaching English without it. "You're beating a dead horse!" complained some students next class, those who could see nothing in rereading. You think this horse is dead? It's panting! It's sweating! It's laid out before you but its heart is pounding! *You think I'm beating it?* Stories, I realized, were like McDonald's wrappers to many of these students—to be emptied and tossed. And I could show them otherwise. I could show them lines to read between, with incandescent meanings clustered there, and sunken compartments in which spirits lay. For the first time in my entire life, I knew I knew something.

After that, I couldn't help but become more attuned to my own internal signs. Was this the beginning of adulthood?—the signals finally making sense? Because the pangs of hope, the jolts of envy, the stinging rasp when mocked—now instead of seeming the nonsensical knocks and pings of life's engine, they rapped out a pattern of obvious significance.

In November my students read the *Metamorphoses*, and walking along the deep green corridor after my class, it occurred to me that Nostradamus was an incarnation of the sacred poet Orpheus. My class had just read that the poet's chopped-off head, floating down the river after he is slain, retains its mystic power: "his tongue, / Lifeless, still murmured sorrow, and the banks / Gave sorrowing reply." Just like the physician/astrologer who continued to prophesy! So, a song is lodged in the body itself! I'd acted as if my own body were in fact a McDonald's wrapper, useful just to keep me intact.

I'd always assumed that the *Creature Feature* prophet was a warning image of the hyperdeveloped mind—as if to be an intellectual, and especially a female intellectual, meant having to foreswear the other ordinary fulfillments: children, sensuality, a normal home life. I thought women had to choose. Now I saw the prophet as someone who traveled between the physical and the metaphysical, which were not unrelated, as I'd assumed. They might even be in communion, might even sometimes be the same. The body— might the body itself actually be a divining rod, of sorts, helping you to find where treasure was buried, help you to understand what things meant?

Still, despite these glimmers of awareness, it was a hard time, that first year I taught. My internal signals kept bringing me into conflict with those I loved. No wonder I hadn't wanted to read them! Now I had to confront the friends who intimidated me, or at least my attraction to them. And I had to confront as well my tendency to put myself second, my assumption I didn't need to be seen—I'd been wrong about that. Another mistake. I *did* need to be seen! I didn't want a curtained life!

The tensions with my boyfriend, in particular, became acute.

"I hope you enjoyed buying those underpants," he'd said with a rigid, panicked smile when I held up a purchase from a lingerie shop.

Because obviously they would have no impact on him.

I'd spent the afternoon among balcony brassieres and merry widows. No, I had not enjoyed it. I'd found the whole expedition mortifying. I'd found my own body mortifying. But wanted something to kindle us, to make what was dead between my boyfriend and me alive again. No go. "I hope you enjoyed buying those underpants"—he'd said, with a stricken, frozen smile.

"How awful," remarked my best friend, in a restaurant the next day.

"Really?" I stared at her.

"Yes!"

But why was I surprised? Hadn't I felt, at the time, awful? But then I'd instantly gone numb. Zoned out. Returned myself to a kind of docility—a refusal to draw conclusions. Which was much easier to endure than the crumpling, aching sadness at knowing I might have to leave my cherished boyfriend.

But that was the problem! *Right there!* Going numb.

I gazed into the candle flame. Well, so what if I left him? I shut my eyes and the candle still burned, although its orange was now green. Why did the thought of leaving him disturb me so much? Wasn't it better to grow angry at his reaction—"I hope you enjoyed buying them!"—than to go dead? Or, wasn't it better to whisper: "Really? Is that all you have to say?"

Anagnorisis is the term for an Aristotelian recognition. It marks the moment in a play when the hero comes to a realization about what he's done, who he is. I read this the next day in the college library while studying *Oedipus Rex*. My study carrel was beside a Gothic window diamonded with chicken wire. The sky was a blue sword burning overhead. Can there be an anagnorisis involving underpants, I wondered, tears in my eyes. Is that too ridiculous?

The philosopher Stanley Cavell, I read on, says that anagnorisis occurs when the hero allows himself an emotional reaction to his intellectual understanding. The two functions had been kept apart during the hero's quest. While Oedipus pursued the truth of his situation, he couldn't allow himself to react. He needed to follow the evidence wherever it led—that great detective who in his youth had solved the riddle of the Sphinx itself. But then: the anagnorisis occurs when he permits the emotional reaction, the inner response to the facts he's unearthed. That's when he goes wild, blinding himself, gouging out his own eyes with the brooches. And it's this very thing—allowing an emotional awareness of what he's done—that Macbeth flees the entire length of his play, leaving a bloody path behind him.

I looked up from my book to the blazing blue arrow tip of sky. So: what changed a person was allowing yourself to feel what you knew. My stomach hurt. I didn't like this answer one bit. My own emotions were still rabid, prone to exaggeration, incessantly misleading. And yet, what else did I have to go by if I ignored them? I'd been waiting for my feelings toward the man I was involved with to change for years, and they hadn't. They only became sharper, more intense. My heart beat so hard, sitting in that library, that the stacks of books jumped away, came back. My moist palms clung to my tissue-thin *Oedipus Rex*. I would almost rather be numb forever than have to talk to my boyfriend about this problem.

I love him, I love him, I told myself as I walked across the battered campus toward home, and felt sicker and more frightened the closer I got to our apartment, but also somehow angrier, too. Had I really been so mysterious? Had he really been so unable to see my unhappiness? Or was he like Stacy somehow, the mean friend, ignoring what was obvious, which was the girl making faces over her shoulder, hurrying up the street both smiling and grimacing?

That night, in bed, I whispered to him, "No, I did not enjoy buying those underpants. And I feel worried about what's wrong between us. I feel unloved, living with you. It's so lonely." Around three or four in the morning he woke me abruptly from a profound sleep, a sleep I'd been sunken so deeply inside it felt like being drunk. "There's something I have to tell you," he intoned in a dull, zombie voice, standing beside the bed, a look of horror on his face. His skin glowed silver in the streetlight. He wove in place, as if about to collapse.

"Tell me right away. You're scaring me!" I said.

He revealed he'd been having an affair. He needed me to know. It was standing in the way of his feeling his love for me. And the words I'd said that night about feeling unloved—they broke his heart! He knew he had to tell me. It was the only way ahead, he felt. It was our only hope of real intimacy. He had to tell me what he'd done, who he was. He stood pale, shaking with fear.

I was shocked and furious—and relieved. At least I no longer felt insane. At least the world again made sense. At least I had all the information, or enough of it.

We sat close. We were both frightened. It was the dawn of something new. "I felt so awful," he told me softly. "So far away from you."

I nodded, sighing. How could I be angry at him (although I was)? For months I'd felt the bone-deep cold within myself. I'd known it without knowing it, his affair, his lack of attraction, the isolation, the sense of being unloved, and I'd swiveled my head the other way, not wanting to see. I'd ignored his secret. I'd kept my complaints weak, I hadn't demanded more. I'd chosen calm and coma, as had he. Now we clenched hands hard across the space between us. We stayed up until the apartment buildings acquired tall peripheries, their rims brightening, sharpening, and the night began to fade to gray, turning the same color as the apartment buildings.

He sat before me, a young man, eager, energetic—as if he'd dropped a weight of years! How different he looked! A beautiful young man, a fawn, with gleaming large eyes and long eyelashes and pointed ears, excited, turned on to me, and I was shocked by my response. He was perfect—for someone else. Perhaps there was something wrong with me, but his eagerness, his freshness, his smiling, doe-eyed glance felt wrong for me. I didn't want it. I felt like some sort of villain. How much he was bringing me! The banquet of his entire eager, undefended self. But he seemed a nubile boy. Oh, I needed to set him free. For it felt just like another kind of blackmail, his radiant eagerness, which asked me not to spoil it. It invited me to go mute again. In fact, his pliant, gentle lips, his doting, wet eyes, his tongue which lay in my own mouth like a sponge—inspired in me a kind of rage.

No more lying. No more zoning out, I told myself. Go with the twists and turns, the blazing maze. Trust that your truth will unlock the other person's. And even if it doesn't, at least it will unlock your own. The living room had grown larger, its corners swabbed with daylight. And, when I looked outside, the buildings no longer stood in hues of monotone gray. My heart beat hard in my chest.

"Oh, baby, I'm so sorry," I began. "It just doesn't work between us. Don't you feel it?"

Soon we were weeping—terrified, and sad to inflict so much pain on one another. We'd been together for years. A sharp awareness of time itself swept in—I felt as if I were inflicting time itself on my boyfriend. "I'm sorry," I said again. But color was seeping into things, the russet brick of the neighboring buildings, the silver zigzag cascade of the fire escapes, and I could finally see, closer, oh, the particular, killing handsomeness of this man before me.

I ultimately left, packing my green camp trunk, lugging down the stairs the old Smith Corona typewriter with its key the size of an eyelash at the end of a string. I drove away in my burgundy VW that had no heat, my body trembling. The windows of stores flashed a sea blue. The sun saturated the sky. Energy that had been trapped in our relationship seemed to have been let loose. I noticed a tree with acorns as big as plums and jagged leaves the size of handkerchiefs. A man on the pavement met my gaze as I waited for a light to change. He was walking a golden retriever. He seemed an intelligent, kind man, somebody's husband. The light turned green and I sped on. When I become involved with someone else, I vowed, I will try not to zone out again, no matter the cost. The key on the typewriter case scratched as the car traveled, swinging and scraping against the nubbled-plastic case. My car took an abrupt turn. There was a moment's pause. Then the little key struck hard before gradually resuming its steady, restless creak. Who was to protect me? I had to trust my own gut sense of things.

Surrendering Oz

I was always stricken, as a child, at the moment when the Wicked Witch in *The Wizard of Oz* cried, "I'm mellllting!" The shocked anguish on her face, the way she crumpled to the floor—guilt overcame me. As much as I'd hated her before, suddenly, to my surprise, remorse washed over me, and painful sympathy: She was my own mother, dissolving!

Quick, she mustn't be let die! Prop her up! A terrible mistake must have been made. And the moment I had expected to feel thrilled triumph (as we would have if this were a boy's story: We're glad the knight slays the dragon) turned out to be spiked with a baffling sense of betrayal. But wasn't the girl supposed to win? Wasn't the Wicked Witch evil? And how had my mother snuck into it all?

The boy's coming-of-age story is about leaving home to save the world. The girl's coming-of-age story is about relinquishing the world beyond home. It is about finding a way to sacrifice one's yearning for the larger world and to be happy about it. At its center is the image of the hungry woman, the desirous, commanding, grasping woman who shows herself, with a blow to our heart, to be the woman we love most.

Or is she?

As a child, I wasn't sure. Watching the witch dissolve, I knew I'd glimpsed something. I was snagged. Distracted. The story stopped for me right there; I was no longer immersed. Because, wasn't one meant to vanquish the dragon? Should one have despised that witch so much? Maybe, maybe . . . and a sort of unraveling happened—one had misunderstood, one had got one's signals crossed, one was too impulsive, eager, girlish. Precisely because it never got looked at—in girls' stories and in my own life the plot rushed on—that unease remained: a suspicion of one's flaring impulses. A tendency to go vague. The sort of dubiousness that makes a student shoot her hand up in class, but then, quite slowly, lower it, and afterward trail home unsettled, head bent.

At a certain point in my own life, everything partook of this same confusion. I had gotten something I craved—a writing contract, a broomstick of my own—only to find, to my dismay, that apparently it wasn't what I'd wanted, after all. I was blocked, locked, grounded. After ten years of writing, suddenly I could not work. Why had my yes turned into a no? How had I learned to be paralyzed? In the absence of any pertinent memory, I found myself obsessed with the great cultural memory of Dorothy in Oz. Besides the moment the witch's face alters, I kept thinking about the scene in which Dorothy is imprisoned in the witch's keep. "Auntie Em!" she cries, in Judy Garland's signature throbbing voice, while Em, in the crystal ball, calls "Dorothy! . . . Where are you? We're trying to find you!" peering and turning and vanishing into Kansas.

"Oh, don't go away," moans Dorothy. But it's too late. How far the daughter has traveled from her mother—into realms unimaginable, like a girl who leaves home for verboten erotic love and can't return, or a daughter whose ambitions transport her far from her mother's values. "Oh, don't go away!" rang in my mind, and my eyes dripped. Locked in my own situation, I identified, not understanding quite why. It was late November, a month since I'd signed the contract, and still no words came, or rather no words came and stayed. I seemed under a spell. I crossed everything out; nothing was what I meant anymore.

I was living at the time in the town of Salem, Massachusetts, on Pickman Street, a narrow, weathered passageway of saltbox houses near Collins Cove. Each morning I hunched at my key-hole desk as if wedged in a kayak. I set down words, then retracted them, ignoring the visitors who strolled past my first-floor window hauling chaise longues to the curve of beach at the end of the street. Even in winter people sunbathed on the mudflats and dug for crabs in shallows that extended for a mile when the tide was out. One late-November dusk after a particularly frustrating day, a day when more words than ever presented themselves but were always the wrong ones, the ones that didn't lead where I needed to go, I abandoned my cross-outs and wandered to the shore.

It looked freshly troweled, it was so smooth. A plump woman lay on a pink lawn chair in the gusting wind, beach towels covering her from toes to chin, eyes fixed on a fluffy-paged bestseller. Beside her on the sand sat a dirty-haired child who glanced up at me with the triangular, sullen, pretty, kittenish face of a minx. I liked her instantly, and smiled. She stuck out her tongue. Then, clasping her red metal shovel, she returned to her labors, digging restively in the sand. There was no one else. The shore was so saturated that it shimmered a reflective sky blue, inducing an upside-down sensation. The low sea here sloped deeper by the most infinitesimal degrees; you could walk out to the horizon, and still be wet only to your knees. Across the muck near my sneakers tiny beasts had dragged unwieldy claws, leaving momentary gnomic communications. It seemed to me for an instant as if the girl herself, isolated beside her mother, bored and in a rage, had forced up onto the sands themselves the thwarted message, this scrambled rune.

I sighed, and the solitary woman glanced up blindly and flipped her page, then continued reading, a Picasso goddess pursuing the gossip of Olympus, incurious about meager mortals. The child heaved a heap of dirt over her shoulder. An oily, metallic tang arrived: rife, fulsome, making my gorge rise. I dug my hands deep into my pockets, and walked back to the sidewalk. When I regained it, I turned. A trail of footprints held the precise waffle grid of my sneakers. Within seconds the prints blurred, though, already beginning to be subsumed by the smooth sand, and inducing a panic within me. I walked quickly home.

The next day was even worse. A headache split my skull. After an hour I thrust the page of cross-outs away and grabbed my coat. I would go to Blockbuster Video. Perhaps seeing the Oz story again would help me understand what was wrong. The day was again cold. It came as a relief, as I shut the door behind me, to step into raw, stinging gray air.

I'd been inside too much. Now I trod hastily past the historic federalist brick manses that framed the town green. A neighborhood realtor in a silk scarf and earrings, her face heavily but expertly powdered, coasted by at the wheel of a Mercedes. Her car seemed not to roll so much as eventually migrate past, bearing clients who gazed steadily out at the museum-like edifices with their hoopskirt chandeliers and ponderous, tasseled curtains. Soon the streets descended. Far beneath us lay the remnants of the town's weary commercial district. Here a Greek-temple-front post office presided over a central parking lot, adjacent to which stood a decaying grocery store that sold iceberg lettuce and tough tomatoes packed three to a box under crackly cellophane, and where, in the aisle, I'd once, memorably, seen a pudgy pink man wearing a T-shirt that read: "Is that your face or did your neck throw up?"

A particular flinty population shared the town. They interested me, as they were so at odds with both the showcase element and the sunny, touristic day-trippers. I had no proper context for them—the Bronx didn't seem to have a precise equivalent. Some of these people (my landlady, a gaunt, quivering woman, among them) often seemed to be seething. Many survived the dark New England hours aided by alcohol. It was not uncommon to see a pallid person rattling a shopping cart piled impressively to the brim with empty beer cans over the cobblestones to the redemption center. Many people had bumper stickers on their old beaters: EXPECT THE RAPTURE. The town, which was becoming ever more discernible to me, had at least four distinct districts—the patrician boulevards lined with the first millionaires' mansions in America, their existence due to the pirating of British ships and to the whaling trade; the funky weather-beaten wood houses huddled by the sea and now subdivided into picturesque if idiosyncratic apartments such as the one I occupied; the underclass of white townies and Dominicans in rotting, ramshackle multistory dwellings behind the Walgreen's; and a new, young, burgeoningly healthful business-school element living in spiffy renovated condos, all permeated by a daily influx and outflow of tourists, and all cheek by jowl. I was always glad to have a reason to walk through; the sheer amplitude was heartening, the sense that there were myriad ways one could live. Now, as I walked, something punitive and exacting—something that seemed to hold life itself as the enemy—eased in me.

The Blockbuster was a vast, blue-carpeted space that seemed to have few videos, and favored the very most recent. Still, it did have what I'd come for. I rented it, and bought a packet of stale, brittle, brilliant orange peanut-butter-and-cheese crackers, then began to wander back through the bluish slate streets, munching as I strolled. An optimism took me—simply from holding the movie. A cardinal perched on a picket fence, I noticed, its triangular crest bright in the gray air. A black-and-white cat with a jingling collar crouched down and then slunk into a busted basement window. I smiled. Somehow I'd been recently myopic, gazing into dull gauze, lost in a troublesome middle distance. Now charming particulars glinted out—the yellow beak of the bird, the hunch of the cat. For an instant I felt as if the world itself were the key to a giant, encoded cipher. That cardinal was both itself and a signifier of something else—something that was, somehow, also only itself, the cardinal. You needed to go no further than what was before your eyes. It was all here.

The truth of the world is inherent richness, I felt. There isn't one right way! I can get where I need to go by myriad paths, myriad sentences—for I suddenly understood that, as soon as I'd received the writing contract, I'd craved to write something truer than I'd written before, something more significant and odd.

This was why my permission had turned to prohibition! There was something more important to me than the book I'd outlined, although I hadn't quite known it earlier. Once I sold the proposal, though, this more important thing, to my surprise, announced itself and demanded expression. It was a relief now finally to realize this. Here was my problem. I momentarily had the mad sensation that the cat had told it to me, and the cardinal. Tomorrow would be different when I sat down to work.

At this thought, a jolly creaking rose to my ears. It had been accompanying me, I suddenly realized, for quite a way. Companionable. Cheery. There it was. *There!* It sounded like the rasping meow of a very old cat. It made me want to dance. I moved my leg, and there was the creak. I stopped, and all was silence. Why, it came from the rollers of the cassette! They were loose, and wobbly, and registered each step, as if I were being accompanied by a companion made of jointed plastic. How goofy! How fun! And this hilarious sound kept me, as I strolled up the cobblestones, merry, dear company all the way home, assuring me that I was not alone, that I ought to be of good cheer, and that tomorrow really would be different.

I woke however to an inhospitable world. The streets were glazed. A freezing rain had fallen overnight, and then the temperatures plunged. Icy air seeped in around the old window casings. I tried to write. My sentences shattered. My stiff, cold fingers seemed to be the problem. I shook them until they batted one another. I held them under the hot water but they wouldn't sufficiently warm. To my dismay, I was still stuck in my writing. In the early afternoon, I let my pen drop. Then I drew the curtains shut, inserted the videotape, and, with a sigh of relief, plumped down to watch *The Wizard of Oz*.

And the movie did let me see, quite soberly, why I was still transfixed. The clues were everywhere. I hadn't watched it in twenty years but my mouth uttered key lines along with the characters. The movie's rhythms were in my body like the pulse of a song that's on the radio so low you don't notice it, yet your feet tap to its beat and you are nodding your head.

Dorothy is racing up the road, all in a frazzle. "Auntie Em!" she cries. "Uncle Henry!" Her little charge, Toto, has gotten into some natural, even hormonal mischief, chasing Miss Gulch's cat. Yet the punishment will be dreadfully severe. It just doesn't seem fair! But Dorothy, a quintessential adolescent, comes off as all elbows and histrionic gasps. She's only in the way. "Dorothy, please! We're trying to count!" her aunt chastises. "Don't bother us now," says Uncle Henry. They're gathering up eggs, and Dorothy will make them lose track. Financial troubles threaten the farm; there's no time for Dorothy's breathless complaints.

The situation is the same with the rest in this dusty, grim world; the farmhands are all busy or give silly, heedless advice. "You going to let that old Gulch heifer buffalo you? Next time she squawks, walk right up to her and spit in her eye. That's what *I'd* do," advises Zeke.

"Aw, you just won't listen, that's all," says Dorothy. Her sense of what's crucial is so different from the adults'. Her aunt seems impatient for Dorothy to grow up and realize what matters (counting eggs; maybe it's time for Dorothy to take notice of her own incipient fertility), to give up childish concerns and take responsibility for the womanliness her body suggests she already possesses. Dorothy wears a pinafore that crams her breasts against her and spills into a frothy white yoke of blouse while every other woman in the movie wears a dress. Dorothy seems to have outgrown her childish frock without noticing, or perhaps she's installed in a sort of transitional training dress, like the training wheels on a bicycle before a child knows how to maintain her balance, or like a "training bra," those concoctions of padding and lace meant to train—not one's breasts, certainly. Well, then, one's mind into an acceptance of one's breasts. Or the boys in one's class into an acceptance of one's acceptability.

How tired Aunt Em looks. One of the characters describes her face as "careworn," as if she'll soon be erased, rubbed away. Perhaps Em would like Dorothy to fill in for her. Instead, the girl frolics, indulging her high spirits. In her exuberance, she tries idly walking the balance beam of the fence top between the animal enclosures, but tumbles right into the hogs' slovenly pen. The big loud beasts start to trample her, and she shrieks. Finally a man rescues her; the other farmhands rush up. Their circle of warm laughter is descended upon by the irate Em.

Dorothy's first fall is due to her carefreeness, her animal high spirits (like Toto, she wanders after "trouble"). Dorothy can't keep her balance; she is not used to the weight of being a woman yet. And her burgeoning, fence-flouting femaleness lands her flat in the mire. The farmhands all come running. She gets them to show concern when Aunt Em won't. Unrescued, though, wouldn't she be a "Miss Gulch"?

The word *gulch* comes from the Middle English word meaning to gulp. It refers to "a deep or precipitous cleft or ravine, especially one occupied by a torrent" and "containing a deposit of gold." The word *gulch* also meant "to swallow or devour greedily," the way a glutton or drunkard might, and the act of "taking a heavy fall."

A woman who is a gulch is a devouring, appetitive, carnal woman, a torrential woman who will swallow you up into her vacuumous cleft. (She recalls Shakespeare's weird sisters on the "blasted heath," that gashed, watery waste whose hags draw their power from arousing taboo cravings.) Kansas's particular Gulch is an aging spinster, which in the era of the movie meant she occupied a certain realm of death—undesired, sterile and thwarted. And yet, unlike Aunt Em, she pays *a lot* of attention to Dorothy.

We know from the start that Miss Gulch is a wanting woman—it is *her* demands that set the world of the movie in motion, that set Dorothy rushing up that road of dust. The very first words of the picture are "She isn't coming yet, Toto. Did she hurt you, Toto? She tried to, didn't she?" with Judy Garland's frightened face staring straight into the camera toward the impending, wrathful She. In fact, the real, scarcely noticed precipitating event is Dorothy's decision to go past Miss Gulch's house on the way home. Couldn't she predict that Toto would once again invade Miss Gulch's garden? When a farmhand suggests she simply choose a different route home, Dorothy exclaims, "You just don't understand." But what exactly doesn't he get? That Dorothy *wants* to explore Miss Gulch's garden?

When we see this appetitive female, she is anything but fat, as we might expect a ravenous "gulch" might be. She flies into the movie on her bicycle (historically the symbol of a liberated woman: the first bikes were made in retooled corset shops, and gave middle-class women freedom of movement; bike makers, in turn, bolted together the first airplanes. Stays to spokes to wings). Miss Gulch is a gnarled skinny vixen stoked with a commanding fury. She trembles with energy. She *will* be satisfied.

Many of the scenes I was most drawn to, incidentally, are in the black-and-white section. These scenes form the back story that impels all the rest. When I watched them on that wintry afternoon, it was with a feeling of eerie unfamiliarity, as if I were seeing a reality that had been hidden in plain view.

"Ga-yle!" trumpets Miss Gulch, saluting Uncle Henry with his last name in perfunctory military fashion. "I want to see you and your wife right away. It's about Dorothy."

Uncle Henry stages a few jokes at Miss Gulch's expense. She says she's here because of Dorothy, but she keeps talking about the dog. She's conflated the two! "Dorothy bit you?" he asks. "She bit her *dog*?"

He blinks, holding a whitewashing brush. He's whitewashing the fence (walls and gates and doors of all sorts figure emphatically here). Miss Gulch claims she's almost lame from where Toto bit her on the leg, but obviously she's lying—she glances down and her face takes on an almost guilty look. Besides, she's nowhere near lame; she's one of the most vigorous, nimble women imaginable. She announces that Toto is "a menace to the community." From the looks of him, he could hardly hurt a flea—he's a yappy, bright-eyed terrier who extends a consoling paw when Dorothy feels blue. In fact, he is the only one who pays much loving attention to Dorothy at all—he is her all, her "toto," her soul, as well as embodying her own instinctive animal spirits.

"He's really gentle. With gentle people, that is," Em points out.

Bizarrely, Miss Gulch *does* seem to have an impulsive shrinking terror of the creature—she drops way back in her chair when he's near. It's as if she fears he might recognize her when no one else does (it's Toto, of course, who later drags the curtain away from the man operating the smoke-and-thunder machine). Dorothy would give up just about everything she has to save him (she proves that when she runs away). Yet Miss Gulch wants to "take him to the sheriff and see that he's destroyed." Why? Out of mere vindictiveness?

"Their magic must be very strong or she wouldn't want them so badly," the good witch later declares about the wicked one's desire for the red shoes. Aunt Em also identifies the issue as power. "Just because you own half the county doesn't mean you have power over the rest of us!" she exclaims.

But Miss Gulch does. She comes equipped with magic: a slip of paper from the sheriff. If they don't give her the dog, she rants, "I'll bring a suit that will take your whole farm. There's a law protecting people from dogs who bite." How fast the dog has transformed into the farm! No one questions this dream logic.

She claps open her basket (it seems like a torture device), and Aunt Em nods to Uncle Henry to pry the pooch from Dorothy, who stares from Henry to Aunt Em, then runs off weeping. Miss Gulch cycles away in triumph, what she wants contained, for the moment at least, in her woven box.

"Boxes, cases, cupboards, and ovens represent the uterus," Freud had noted in what now seems an almost cartoonishly reductive analysis and yet one still pertinent in this context. Miss Gulch has Dorothy's genie, her wild pleasure, caged up for herself. But her lock can't keep Toto; her basket is not secure. Toto pushes free and gallops back to his rightful mistress.

This is a story about who owns what, about merging and splitting and boundaries, about the right to consolidate or not to consolidate one's sovereign identity, as archetypal stories about women generally are. Historically disempowered, taught to exercise boundless empathy, women's drama often enacts the story of the self absconded with—ravished, raped, invaded and annexed. Demeter and Persephone, Hera and Io, Cinderella, Snow White, Sleeping Beauty, all are about self-possession and the struggle with a rapacious outside force. The Oz story, too, has to do with the control of one's own animating spirit.

Toto leaps in Dorothy's window (the window is one image for the mind here) and she embraces him. Quick, she realizes, "they" will be back: Her own home is in league with "them" (Aunt Em doesn't even consider challenging the sheriff's order or explaining her viewpoint to this invisible, commanding man. As with Oz's diplomas, what's on paper holds supreme magic). Dorothy heaves her suitcase onto her bed. She will run away.

Frog or dragon figures often begin archetypal stories, according to Joseph Campbell. "The disgusting and rejected frog or dragon of the fairy tale," he writes, "is representative of that unconscious deep wherein are hoarded all the rejected, unadmitted, unrecognized, unknown, or undeveloped factors, laws, and elements of existence. . . . Those are the nuggets in the gold hoard of the dragon."

What is Miss Gulch's specific gold? The powers locked inside Dorothy that are yet unknown. Miss Gulch reveals Dorothy's home's fragility, its inability to keep Dorothy content; it is so much whitewash and cardboard before this woman's roar. "Then I'll huff and I'll puff. . . ." Miss Gulch sets Dorothy on her way.

At the end of a long, dry road, when Dorothy is merely a lonely figure, vulnerable and fatigued, she happens upon a caravan. It proclaims the presence of the celebrated Professor Marvel. The man is camped under a bridge, like the proverbial gnome. Clad in a threadbare cutaway and frilled shirt, and roasting wieners like a hobo, this fancy gentleman is obviously a fraud. Yet before Dorothy utters hardly a word, he gazes at her and proclaims that she is running away because "They don't understand you at home. They don't appreciate you. You want to see other lands. Big cities, big mountains, big oceans."

"Why, it's like you could read what's inside me," she exclaims.

So her motive isn't just to save Toto! Or, perhaps her two aims are one: To save her animal spirit, she must go out into the world. She is one of a long tradition of midwesterners who want to come east to college or west to make his fortune—to leave behind the consuming farm.

Discussing why women through history hardly ever wrote, and why, when they did, they rarely achieved the free flight of genius granted men, Virginia Woolf invokes women's confined experience. Women were kept home, and ignorant. "Anybody may blame me who likes," she quotes Jane Eyre as saying. And why does Miss Eyre feel justifiably open to blame? Because she climbs up on the roof while the housekeeper makes jellies in order to look past the fields to see the more distant view.

Jane Eyre longs for "a power of vision which might overpass that limit; which might reach the busy world, town, regions full of life I had heard of but never seen . . . practical experience. . . . It is narrow-minded in their more privileged fellow-creatures to say [women] ought to confine themselves to making puddings and embroidery bags." Suddenly, though, in the midst of these thoughts, Miss Eyre is called back by Grace Poole's mad laugh. It is like being interrupted, as Dorothy (whose last name also refers to air) so often is at the giddy height of her happiness, by the mocking glee of Elvira Gulch: the cackle of a woman who flew off over the horizon.

"Ah," remarks the professor when Dorothy is amazed by his grasp of her innermost wishes. "Professor Marvel doesn't guess. He *knows*." He likely recognizes something of himself in her. But, a responsible gate guardian, he contrives to send her home. How?

He will read his crystal ball, he announces. He dons a turban with a central jewel reminiscent of the circular mirror doctors once wore above their eyes to help see inside you. He swipes from inside Dorothy's basket a photo and looks at it in secret. Here are the girl and her aunt side by side at their front gate, smiling, both wearing fancy ironed dresses. It is a posed picture—a startling photo, and it takes a moment to realize why. In all the scenes until now, not once have we seen Mrs. Gale actually looking happy.

The professor gazes into the cloudy ball. He does what his sign promised he could do. He reads her "Past, Present, and Future in His Crystal."

He sees an older woman in a polka dot dress, he says. She has a careworn face. She's crying, he says. "Someone has hurt her. Someone has just about broken her heart."

"Me?" Dorothy asks.

"Well, it's someone she loves very much. Someone she's been very kind to, taken care of in sickness."

"I had the measles once. She stayed right by me every minute."

"She's putting her hand on her heart. What's this?! She's dropping down on the bed. Oh, the crystal's gone down!"

Dorothy leaps up. Her independence, it seems, will kill the woman who sacrificed herself, who allowed her own face to be worn away—who effaced herself—for Dorothy, the woman who literally *runs* about the farm from chore to chore. Why, she *chose* to be Dorothy's mother when she didn't have to (she's Aunt Em— Aunt Mother. The use of mother surrogates in fairy tales, of course, allows the more frightening emotions to surface).

How weak Aunt Em suddenly appears! Before now, she's been a powerhouse. It's as if, in leaving, Dorothy stole *her* Toto, her soul. To have the world, apparently, the girl must steal herself from her mother. It's tantamount to seizing the cornerstone of a house—the other person topples.

Rapunzel flees her mother's prison tower and becomes an exile. For seven years she and her beau live in a Sahara. Devoid of mother, the world is punitive, desolate as the winter earth is when Persephone keeps her yearly liaison. Iciness is the punishment for sex: for each pomegranate seed the daughter savored, the mother bestows a frozen month.

Luke Skywalker, in comparison, is evicted. His family home is destroyed so *that* he'll be forced to assume his manhood duties. He must relinquish home to save the world, like Hamlet or Superman, both of whom experience the destruction of their childhood abodes: they are thrust out to make the world right. Men leave home to restore it. If they don't depart, sickness and rot result. Even the far more recent *Sunset Boulevard*, which depicts a young man who lives in what is symbolically the narcissistic mother's mansion, selling his soul for a gold cigarette case, is about inner decay. The Graduate returns to his childhood home only to be corrupted by the parental femme fatale: he must go forth. Young men must give up home or home will sicken.

The professor reads Dorothy's fears and knows just when to stop—at the brink of the unthinkable. The crystal's gone down.

"I thought you were coming with me!" the wandering man says in mock surprise.

"I have to get to her right away," Dorothy cries as she flees.

And now a curious thing happens. A tornado gusts up. Nobody seems to have predicted this. And the farm now really is in jeopardy. It's not from Miss Gulch this time or because Dorothy is running away, but because Dorothy is coming back.

How does it feel to have to sacrifice the entire world for a parent's happiness? Quite a squall is brewing. A twister is coming, in which everything—all objects, all meanings—will get twisted. It whirls across the horizon, a dark ascending coil like the probing mouth of a vacuum cleaner. The horizon is inhaled. Aunt Em, Uncle Henry, and the farmhands vanish down into the storm cellar. Dorothy returns to a deserted house. She stamps on the door to the cellar; they won't open up. They have walked down into the underworld, marched into a grave in the earth. In fact, this too may hold an unconscious wish: If they abandoned her, she would not have to feel guilty about abandoning them.

On the surface, though, Dorothy's sudden solitude terrifies. Trees wrench up their roots and sail aloft. The front screen door blows off in her hand. "Aunt Em!" she cries. In a twist, her own life is now in peril. The house is what Elvira Gulch implied: balsa and paint, like the court in which Queens and Kings judged Alice in Wonderland only to watch Alice surge bigger and bigger until she declares, "Why you're just a pack of cards!" while they whirl away.

But Dorothy's return home might literally cost her her life: The house attacks. The frame of her window (her own crystal) smashes her on the head. She swoons onto her bed. All at once a peaceful expression comes over her. Her face doubles into an overlay and an underlay; the twin images superimpose over one another, seesaw through each other, brows, noses, smiles nodding up and down, agreeing to something marvelous.

In Dorothy's delicious dream her house sails high. It is a doll's house, a toy house, although when it comes down to earth its landing is real enough: It kills. Dorothy's first act in this new sublimity is to crush a faceless woman. "She's gone where the gardens grow. Below, below, below," just like Aunt Em. Of course, it's an accident. But, as the Wicked Witch drolly observes: "I can cause accidents too, you know." (Ironically, this is precisely what finishes her off: She incites an accident that dissolves her. Dorothy is capable of violence, apparently, only under the guise of an accident.) The murder implement of this first act? It's death by house, as if the incarnated burden of housework could be hurled like a thunderbolt.

Yet, ring the bell! This is cause for celebration. The wicked old witch at last is dead! Who is this witch? Well, we can't quite see yet; nothing is visible but her feet on which gleam the scarlet power slippers.

Shoes figure in other archetypal women's tales. In *Cinderella* they unlock the secret of the heroine's identity and liberate her from servitude; at the end of *Snow White* the evil queen dances in fiery metal heels as punishment for her blazing passions. In *The Red Shoes* they curse the wearer to live out the restless, driven, vagabond existence of the artist, which is portrayed as incompatible with settled married love. Cuplike, snug, shoes are an emblem of sexual power—which is something to be either punished or celebrated, as the case may be. How significant that the totalitarian Imelda Marcos assembled a veritable empire of footwear, and that Marla Maples, Donald Trump's faux-royal bride, returned to the tabloids over the theft of a trove of high heels.

When the ruby slippers are popped off, the dead woman's eensy feet curl like party favors. Her peppermint-striped stockinged legs swiftly retract under the house—the woman's gone; the house subsumed her. Her sister, however, arrives, summoned, it seems, by the other's death, or—could it be?—by Dorothy's joy.

Like the dour Em who descends the instant Dorothy and the farmhands are all laughing, the Wicked Witch always appears at the height of Dorothy's festivities. And what are the festivities? The girl from Kansas is being celebrated as the national heroine of a land peopled by adults the size of children, adults who sing songs (in Kansas, Dorothy was the only one who sang), adults who hang on Dorothy's every word and then repeat them to one another as she recounts the story of the ride that made her a sort of Abraham Lincoln to this race who will henceforth regard the time she fell (How liberating it is to fall!) as "A day of independence for all the munchkins and their descendants."

In this dream all her wishes have been fulfilled. Here they understand her. Here they appreciate her (and how!). In the background rise giant mountains. And in the foreground—the colors!

Pinks of incandescent hue, paint-box oranges, plant leaves that gleam like lollipops, and all traversed by a river the Dippity-Do blue of a millionaire's pool. And here a woman in a billowing white gown like an ambulatory cloud and with a voice like a trilling flute floats down in a bubble with words of welcome.

Glinda, the only witch with a name, is a vision of celestial femininity, clean and blonde as can be, and swathed in gossamer layers of veil. She speaks in a baby-doll voice that's high and cloying, a soprano on helium, a woman with a throat so constricted she can only trill. When I was a child, Glinda seemed more of a fraud to me than any of the other characters. She frightened me. Could I ever be her? Impossible as being Tinker Bell or Jo or Julie Andrews as a nun. These women were perfectly clean. "P.U.," I thought when Glinda spoke, my girlhood response when threatened by ultrafemininity.

It is Glinda who sets Dorothy on her yearning, winding way to Oz even though she knows from the outset that Dorothy has the power to go home now, if she'll only click her heels. But wait. I'm wrong. For the shoes to work, Glinda explains, Dorothy must believe they will. There's no point in even trying to reach home until she's learned a particular psychological lesson.

And from the outset, from the *outset*, she wants to go home. As a child this baffled me. What was the matter with the girl? Why was she so pathetically homesick? Couldn't she have any fun? Even watching it as an adult it seemed sad. Oz is a place for *her*. It is sensually delicious, full of magic, play, and song. Dorothy never names the witch as the reason she wants home. As Dorothy weeps outside the shut gates to the Wizard (and these are the words that make the locked doors swing wide, this is her liberating "Open Sesame"): "Auntie Em was so good to me and I never appreciated it. . . . She may be dying, and it's all my fault. I'll never forgive myself—never, never, never, never."

How you gonna keep 'em down on the farm? See under: Oz. The word "Oz," in fact, stands for the second half of the alphabet. Frank Baum was wondering what to call the magical land when he saw his filing cabinet, divided A–N and O–Z. Dorothy gives up half of everything in giving up Oz.

The quest is about reversal. Em didn't really fall on the bed, clutching her heart. Dorothy did; her frame of mind attacked her. Aunt Em has run away, vanishing into the earth, thus flinging Dorothy into the sky. How to restore the balance? Instead of satisfying her own need for appreciation, Dorothy needs to appreciate Em.

"I had an Aunt Em too, you know," says the weeping gate-guardian, swinging open the door to Oz.

The prodigal son is the father's favorite, but the prodigal daughter is considered selfish. This answers the question of why Dorothy wants home so fast. Oz is guilt-stricken exile, without a mother's love. The solution is to choose A–N, the land of definite, particular, pragmatic articles: an egg, an acre, an aunt, the land of factuality, not profligate Ozymandias.

But not until Dorothy believes she deserves Em can she have her back. Em is the Toto now, locked away. To earn her, Dorothy must spin her anger into guilt. She must convert her desire for the world to the desire for home.

"The pure products of America go crazy," wrote Dr. William Carlos Williams, on good authority.

"I'm afraid you've made rather an enemy out of the Wicked Witch," Glinda remarks with an airy nonchalance, although it was Glinda herself who stuck the glitter shoes on Dorothy's feet. Why ensure that Dorothy can't live peacefully with the Witch of the West?

A person becomes taboo "for the simple reason that he is in a condition which has the property of inciting the forbidden desires

of others and awakening the ambivalent conflict in them," Freud[*]
observes. There's something mighty compelling about the woman
who flies on her own stick, keeping in her thrall men whom she
uses for her own devices and beasts like boys that flock at her com-
mand. All this power might *attract* Dorothy, so best make that
woman her enemy from the start.

"You must prove yourselves worthy," Oz roars, and then sets
a test that renders the Wicked Witch an enemy once again. He
himself is lodged at the end of a glistening red hallway, a passage of
ribbed arches like a gallery of wishbones: scarlet, internal, echoey.
Oz is aim and obstacle. Egg-like, legless, with an ample cranium
that presages Marvel's balloon, he hovers, a floating head thronged
with salvers of green smoke and flames like an incarnation of Kubla
Khan's "ancestral voices prophesying war." Dorothy has ascended
into the fomenting, highly defended throne of the Mind-King. He
tells her in effect that she will prove herself worthy of home when
she destroys the Wicked Witch (When he hears that Dorothy must
bring the witch's broom, the smart Scarecrow exclaims: "We'll have
to kill her first!")

Who is this witch? She is a woman who wants. She furnishes
the obstacles to Dorothy's quest—the malicious trees, the soporific
fields. In fact, the whole place sometimes seems to exist in her control: As Dorothy and her new friends sing and stroll blithely along,
she watches them in her ball. The world is her paperweight. What
do we actually know about her? She is thin and green, painted with
the brush of mortality and envy. Something in her is already rotting.
She is friendless, all who attend her enslaved by a spell.

---

[*] Dear Freud, the intellectual papa who first introduced me to the labyrinth of the
psyche, the occurrence of the negative that contains tucked within itself positive and
negative both, and the truth of ambivalence, with its admixture of love and hate, has
never been rendered moot, it seems to me, when it comes to our understanding of the
internal life, even as his flaws and his own analytic fantasies come to light.

"It's so kind of you to visit me in my loneliness," she croons when Dorothy, kidnapped, arrives into her rocky fortress—and despite the sarcasm, her words are poignant. Surrounded by robotic men, attempting to warm herself with a million flickering fires, wouldn't she actually enjoy a daughter? "My pretty," she calls Dorothy, a term of droll cherishing. With her face thin as a chisel, her raggedy black dress binding her bony waist, she looks broken. The pieces of her jut in the fractured angles of a stovepipe rather than flowing in ample round maternal shapes. She is a sort of vicious pauper.

If the witch had the shoes, Dorothy is warned, the witch's power would be absolute. Dorothy's power is her ability to inspire love. If the Wicked Witch had this while she retained her own controlling will, wouldn't she have everything?

Across the very sky, writ in giant charred letters, the witch spells "Surrender Dorothy." Not surrender the shoes but surrender yourself.

The drama of the daughter's journey is: Who will control her? Will she celebrate her own stubborn, lonely will, or will she become a selfless woman, freed from isolation? Locked in the witch's keep, she calls out to Aunt Em like the runaway Jonah crying from the whale where, as he put it, "the earth with her bars closed upon me."

"I'm frightened, Aunt Em! I'm frightened!" She sounds as if she is admitting something she's withheld at long, long last. The world of willful independence is too much for her! Her bravery is at an end.

At once Em appears in the crystal, calling, "Dorothy! It's me! It's Aunt Em. Where are you? We're trying to find you!"

"I'm here in Oz, Aunt Em," cries Dorothy. "I'm trying to get home to you. Oh, *don't* go away!" for already Em is clouding and darkening and twisting until she reveals herself to be—with a shock—the gloating Wicked Witch.

"I'll give you Auntie Em, my pretty!" she sneers.

And doesn't she? When I thought about Em before this, I remembered a kind, loving woman. Yet viewing the movie as an adult, I noticed how grim Em is, and how sharply nasty she can be.

"What's all this jabberwocking about when there's work to be done?" Em demands, implying that the daydreaming that Alice was partial to through the looking glass will not be countenanced here. 'Twas brillig and the slithy toves, indeed!

"I know three shiftless farmhands who'll be out of a job before they know it," she continues.

One explains. "Well, Dorothy was walking along—"

"I saw you tinkering with that contraption, Hickory," she practically spits. "Now get back to that wagon."

Contraptions and tinkering! It's almost as bad as jabberwocking.

"All right, Mrs. G," he replies. He lifts a finger in the air. "But one day they're going to erect a statue for me in this town—"

"Well, don't start posing for it now!" she cuts.

Even when she offers the farmhands a tray of phallic crullers she holds at waist height, it's because "you can't work on an empty stomach."

"You got my finger!" Hank exclaims when the flatbed of a cart is lowered on his helping hand.

Rakes, fingers, and crullers; incubators and wagons—the farm is a suggestive place, and what it suggests to Em is work and more work.

In contrast, the principle of the Emerald City is idleness. "We get up at twelve and start to work by one. Take an hour for lunch and then by two we're done. Jolly good fun!" sing the urbanites. Dorothy, who also loves freedom, liberates as she goes. She unhooks the Scarecrow from his nail, oils the Tin Man where he's rusted (Hickory wanted to have a statue? Fine, the witch has made him one), and cajoles along the Lion.

The men of Oz are all missing one key organ (the Lion wants "the nerve!"). One suspects that, in Dorothy's mind, the men on Aunt Em's farm all lack an organ, too. The farmhands are embodied in the galley slaves whose long-proboscised faces mirror that of the Wicked Witch (these people almost have an *extra* organ). They are cruel to Dorothy only because they are under a spell. In Dorothy's dream, the farmhands appear in both their defiant and their servile incarnations.

Far from being a doting mom, Mrs. Gale comes across as an iron-gray matron who knows quite well, thank you, how to lay down the law. Which is why it comes as a shock when she appears so terribly fragile as soon as Dorothy attempts to leave.

From the start of the movie, Aunt Em is angry. She is *furious*. Is she envious of Dorothy's ability to daydream and sing while she herself is shackled to the farm? Is she jealous of the girl's beauty and fertility (why doesn't Em have children)? Perhaps she is angry simply because there is so much from which she must protect Dorothy.

Dorothy's unbridled growth ruptures the old unity with Em. "Who killed my sister?" Em demands in her witch incarnation. In Dorothy's nightmare vision, Em stretches long fingers toward her, an ugly, voracious starveling. She can pursue Dorothy anywhere. Why, she even appeared when Dorothy ran clear across the country and into the carnie man's tent!

Em stalks Dorothy. The terrifying hourglass the witch overturns resembles a voluptuous scarlet woman draining red dust, a kind of pulverized menstruation. If only Em could remove Dorothy's womanliness—those shoes!—the old joy would be restored. If only Dorothy could give Em back some years, she wouldn't need to feel so guilty. ("This old incubator's gone bad," Uncle Henry reports. The ashen menopausal farm can't sustain its eggs.) "Give them back to me!" cries the Wicked Witch when she sees the ruby shoes on Dorothy's feet. They were hers once. "Give them *back!*" she insists.

But they are time, sexiness, red-mouthed beauty (Dorothy's lush lips are the first thing one notices in color). "Keep tight inside them," Glinda cautions. "Never let them off your feet."

And yet of course one's body does loosen and slip. Time is the movie's true villain, in fact. The film begins mythically, with a scroll of words which names time as the enemy: "For nearly forty years this story has given faithful service to the Young in Heart; and Time has been powerless to put its kindly philosophy out of fashion."

By faithfully serving her mother, a daughter might deny the pull of time, a force like mitosis, when a cell's twin nuclei fling in polar directions, although it will mean remaining childish. In seeing her mother, in fact, a girl often sees herself plus time. Can't the daughter restore to the mother what she herself has apparently devoured? Mother and daughter drain into each other like halves of an "ourglass," two crystals merged, two minds fused. How can they separate? Or, should they just not?

"Why didn't you tell Dorothy earlier that she just needed to tap her heels?" the Scarecrow demands at the end.

"She wouldn't have believed me," says Glinda neatly. "She had to learn something for herself first."

Which is?

"It's that . . . it wasn't enough just to want to see Uncle Henry and Aunt Em. It's that—if I ever go looking for my heart's desire again, I won't go further than my own backyard. Because if it isn't there, I never lost it in the first place."

There. The daughter must not come home resentfully. That might destroy home, much as the caged woman in Rochester's attic and the chained woman in Roderick Usher's basement finally burn down their mansions. She must choose home happily.

"Think to yourself, 'There's no place like home,'" Glinda instructs.

Dorothy shakes her head from side to side as if to say no to Oz, no to Oz, and murmurs the words hypnotically, casting a spell over herself: "There's no place like home." Her whole family appears.

No place like home. For men, the situation is different. Home and world aren't alternatives. Men get to have both. Odysseus leaves to fight and to find adventure knowing home waits (and waits!). Men go and are loved. They are in fact loved more for going: That's brave. Penelope weaves and unweaves. Her calendar is filled and unfilled. Her maturity passes in a kind of temporal trance. Those who aren't content to wait, like Agamemnon's wife, are monsters.

"We thought for a moment she was going to leave us," Uncle Henry says.

"But I did leave—"

"Lie quiet now," Em interrupts. "You just had a bad dream."

"But it wasn't a dream. It was a place . . ."

"Sometimes we dream lots of silly things when—"

"No, Aunt Em, it really existed. . . . Doesn't anyone believe me?"

But then Em shifts. "Of course, we believe you, Dorothy."

And, for an instant, Em does seem to believe, although it's not clear exactly what. That the experience seemed true for Dorothy? Or perhaps, beyond even that, that the land of imaginative delight actually does exist, is real, a place that can be reached? For one extraordinary moment this seems the case.

Dorothy, thrilled to be back, smiles at Em's beaming face, the two happy with each other at long last. Maybe Em wanted to trust all along in Dorothy's "jabberwocking"; maybe she secretly cherishes what she feels impelled to mock. Maybe dreaming might even help her, too.

But Dorothy's not dreaming any more, she vows. "I'm not going away ever, ever again. Oh, Auntie Em," she cries in her final declaration of love to the woman for whom she quested for so long and with such success: "There's no place like home."

Isn't there, I muttered aloud, clicking off the VCR. I flopped back in my chair. At once the afternoon closed in. Oh, it had felt marvelous to be in Oz!, far from the problem of not being able to write. I got up abruptly and swept open the gauze curtains onto a frosty afternoon. A thump came from upstairs, and I glanced up, glowering. The wood-frame house I occupied was so antique and brittle that when the two women who resided on the top stepped across their floor my own apartment pounded. Still, I loved the place. French doors swung between the various rooms and, especially in the summer, when my husband and I moved in, light prismed and refracted throughout. There was a gigantic fireplace in the bedroom and one in the living room, and I built such blazes when the weather changed in mid-September that once the paint bubbled on the mantelpiece and dripped onto the brick. I didn't know that the ideal was a steady, warm, glow; I recalled the fires of my old Girl Scout camp and bought marshmallows. We toasted them on sticks. I was just learning how to live away from the Bronx.

Now, outside, the day was as gauzy gray as if I were still peering through the curtains. The yard and the house behind it remained hazy, ephemeral, the last faint image on an Etch A Sketch that has been repeatedly shaken. When would I be able to function again? And I'd just spent the afternoon not even trying to work.

Guilt cut me, and I snatched my coat and rushed out the back door and into the late-autumn yard, eager to feel the chill after the house's warmth. Ice crackled under my feet. A brittle glitter had formed on the unraked leaves. There was a locust tree clothed in yellow-gold tatters and an ancient walnut tree whose twirling, dangling, carob-like pods I loved to examine—each pod clasped seeds that pressed out through the leathery casing like pearl buttons down the back of a dress or like cruelly protruding vertebrae on an anorexic. The whole place aroused interest; we didn't have private gardens in the Bronx.

This one's most extraordinary feature, however, was a rose bush with saffron-peach floribunda flowers that had turned rusty apricot as winter approached. Each bloated bloom lolled, a silken bell. I'd never lived with a rose bush before. It possessed an almost painful beauty, a loveliness that was like a high-pitched sound behind everything, issuing a demand. For the exquisite, tattered blossoms—maternal somehow—deserved to be registered, celebrated. But it was beyond my power to register them sufficiently. Some were hidden by others; some had fallen to the yellow grass before I'd quite noticed them bloom. All sorts of beauty was going to waste.

My feet had begun to ache from the cold but I didn't want to go in. I hiked back to the rear of the garden, over the crackling icicle grass. Images from the movie lingered. I couldn't depart into my work because I thought my impulses would land me in muck. I had strayed somehow into a zone past my mother's approval, and felt frozen, imprisoned there. I was supposed to be helping my mother—taking care of her in her loneliness and increasing age—but was not. Rabid things in me, irrational things in me, wanted expression, and I was trapped between my obligation to express them and my terror of never being able to return home if I did. I would lose the decency and love of home if I said what I had in me—I would not deserve home. I would be outcast, as, in fact, I already experienced myself to be. I inhabited a frozen world because I had withdrawn approval from myself. In the movie, Dorothy cries out to the witch/aunt/mother, "I'm frightened!" This was the cry that I'd heard in my ears all autumn. Now I understood: the daughter is admitting defeat to the figure who has withdrawn herself. Come back, I'll be good!, she seems to be saying. But I could not be good, apparently. For I wanted to go ahead, not back.

By now my feet had grown so cold that the bones in my little toe felt rigid, obtruding like a chicken's digit. My ears stung. Still, I'd arrived at the prettiest spot in the back of the garden, the willow that presided over the rear of the place with its flickering static deluge of minnow-like yellow leaves.

A hammock was strung between the willow and an oak. How surprising that it was still out! My husband had whiled away many an August afternoon in it, reading. Each strand of webbing was sheathed in bluish ice. It looked as if we'd neglected to put away summer itself. Still, I drew the hammock toward me, then lowered myself in, sitting up. I lifted my legs. Away flew the world—with a sound of cracking ice! I laughed. And stump-walked forward, knees deeply bent. Then I flicked back my toes and gave another kick. Whee! No, I didn't want to write the book I'd proposed, because it now seemed glib. I wanted to delve beyond what I knew merely intellectually, into back gardens of blue tree trunks and seedpods and humus scent and floribunda hillocks—my own Oz world of significance—and to discern the secret patterns. I wanted the line of the essay to lead me there. Any other way ahead now seemed pro forma, empty, soulless as the stately houses on the green. I had to give up the old method, the old map—but it was gone already—in order to find my way into what had real significance.

The rope creaked against the tree trunk. The bright world careened. I no longer felt tense, at all. I felt glorious! Suddenly I drew up my legs, swiveled, and lay down full length in the hammock. The snipped sky raced down, or I'd been shot up in the air. I seem to be resting high up in the leafy branches. Then I thrust one leg onto the ground and pushed, and the rope made a wet flopping sound as it struck the trunk, before it shimmied down along the bark, grinding. How long could I stay out?

For, from my view at the back of the garden, the house itself was obviously the problem, with its tight little square of yellow light, its stuffy aroma of forced heat, its aura of willed effort. If only I could stay out! Somewhere, no, everywhere in this wild ragtag beauty, it seemed, my writing resided: in the flashing cutouts of sky between the bronze leaves, in the leathery seedpods with their string of *o*'s that resembled opposite things at once (wedding gown, anorexic spine), in the miraculously symmetrical, disturbingly lightweight pavilion in which hornets bred in the upper corners of the porch, in the out-of-season, relentless rosebush. It came to me that I wanted to locate and repossess what had been unconsciously projected everywhere. If only I could read the language of jagged spaces, the broken alphabet in the leaf clutter.

I wanted to explore the dirty, forbidden, neglected spaces where my own truths lay gathered, the flinty, irate, incensed, feral strain in my own self. But, wonder of wonders, these were also my own mother's forbidden spaces, it now occurred to me. Her own mother had been strict, frightened, and enslaved to her seamstress work—imposing a great loneliness. Even now my mother carried an air of profound isolation, of friendlessness. In her twenties my mother craved to leave the Bronx for an apartment in Manhattan— but her mother screamed at the notion. Only tramps did that. So my mother stayed home, thwarted. I would have liked to register her beauty so that she too truly felt it, and was satisfied, but I needed to depart.

Did all daughters feel they'd stolen from their mother something they wished they could restore? Still, it occurred to me, as I pushed off with my leg again, maybe one didn't need to trade off between mother and self, finally. Maybe it was a false choice. Maybe you could tell both stories at once, for my mother's truth seemed tucked inside mine.

I gazed from the hammock to the house. So, I thought, Dorothy was right, after all. What you desire is no further than your own backyard, although for some of us that backyard is overgrown and untended.

I stayed out so long that afternoon that all night afterward my ears ached. Next morning at my keyhole desk, though, I still didn't know how to accept what appeared on my page. Well, I thought, if my writing has been stolen, somebody must have the ability to restore it.

Someone did have that ability, as it happened, a psychotherapist. She allowed me to feel that my impulses were shot through with their own internal coherence—a person couldn't help but make sense. And she also let me feel that I could leave her and not lose her approval. She accepted my muck and my celestial glimmers, my envy, dependence, stubbornness, and idolization; she was both Good Witch and Wicked Witch both. And when I truly departed her at last, I did not have to leave behind what she had given me. I'd tucked it within myself. There are many places like home, I learned. The world is full of them.

SABOTAGE

Every morning when I was in my mid-twenties I worked on a novel, and in the afternoon I worked as a secretary in an insurance agency. To get to my afternoon job I had to walk through the Prudential Center, a great big gateway to the city. And every afternoon as I stepped through this gateway I stopped in at a bookstore and found a particular book. This book had recently come out to rave reviews. It was set in Hawaii and was written in lush, lyrical prose. On the back was the author's photo. How composed and lovely she seemed!

As I slid the book back on the shelf, my hand felt numb and tingly. My whole body seemed robotic, hollow, scooped out by envy. I felt … unreal. Then I continued on my way into the city. All the excited, thrilled feelings from my own writing were banished. When I set my shoe on the sidewalk it was just a strange, dull, far-away shoe. Soon I was enclosed in my airless, glass-enclosed office, filing away insurance forms.

What is envy, I started to wonder. And why did I feel a strong urge to look at a book guaranteed to give me a bad feeling? Every compulsion, after all, has its reason.

I was most susceptible to my urge to go into the bookstore when I felt good from writing. The good feeling, I realized, gave me a sense of being strong, and I felt I ought to do something with my strength. Now that I was strong I had no excuse for not looking at that other woman's book. It was an attraction like magnets: I felt positive, the book was negative to me, but I experienced an almost puritanical obligation to learn from it what I could. And what I wanted to learn from it was, do I have a right to feel good about myself? Am I being a fool to feel good, considering what I just wrote?

Because in fact, striding out the door to my afternoon job I felt good, elated, euphoric, almost heliumish. But back when I was a girl we talked about other girls who were "really conceited." I didn't want to appear like a fool, arms flung out like some trumpeting Ethel Merman hogging the stage. I stopped in at the envy store to protect myself. I made myself unreal to counteract the vivid aliveness I felt from writing and which I associated with being excessive and exposed.

I'd grown up in the Bronx with a spectacular but domineering older sister. She dressed in fashionable brown-and-gold muumuus and handmade orange ponchos, and she decorated the margins of her school notebooks with cartoon drawings she sketched with a Waterman pen dipped in jade ink. She was six years older than I, an energetic, heavyset girl with few friends. She liked to put a finger on my mistakes, and wherever she put a finger, my mistakes flourished. "Too much blue," she said of a painting. "Look how cockeyed," she observed of a sorry, peculiar clutch purse with a monocle-sized button that I spent all of seventh grade knitting for a class.

The thing *was* askew, its bottom edge veering dramatically up while the top edge stayed flat, and in one corner the loops lolling as big as wedding rings while elsewhere they were tiny as Sen-Sen. Working on it, I had been divided between despair and boredom, but had maintained the belief that at the last instant, by some magical achievement of "blocking," the purse might be transformed into something beautiful—an opera bag! Anita accurately observed that it had not. Her own stitches were uniform and steady, and, to keep herself amused, she chose patterns that required her often to switch her stitch. In the evening, the tick of her needles rang like the song of cicadas; she knit while she read, her eyes not leaving the textbook as she extended a long arm and drew toward her the next full yard of wool from the ball, which bounced in its bag. I yearned to become like Anita—she was my "after"—but remained Bonnie, the "before."

And yet when I finally lived far away from her in Boston I started to alter. For the first time in my life, I had a room to myself. I shared a freezing, mouse-visited apartment with an actress and a dancer, each of us having a private chamber off a long corridor. The chapters of my novel accumulated; insights glittered up from the pages as if channeled from mysterious spheres. I dashed out of my apartment at twelve thirty to go to my insurance office job, and a flock of pigeons flapped blue-and-silver wings aloft over Huntington Avenue, and, as I hurried past the Red Line T station one day, a ragged old woman asked me if she could have the peach I was in the very midst of eating. I set it in her hand, and within myself I felt stories forming, an excitement surging—and a shaft of fear.

Because it was strange actually to feel I might have something valuable inside me. I didn't want to delude. The bookstore of envy returned me to my sister, to my family, to the comfort of who I'd been. In this way I had become Anita, saying "too much blue," saying "Look how cockeyed." In the absence of the real Anita, I visited the Prudential shop with its book-jacket photo of a woman who wrote skeins unlike anything I might achieve. I wrote Bronx; this book was the tropics. I wrote blatant; this was pastel. Peering into this book was like looking in a bad mirror: I could never find myself.

Or rather, I did, but it was my old self, my blah self, the self I'd desperately craved to leave behind. Here she was! The glossy photo, quick as magic, conjured her. And stoked my hunger for a transformation, making it more dangerous. Today was not the first day of the rest of my life. Okay. Then tomorrow had better be.

How many of us, I began to wonder, cast upon ourselves a similar spell? How many of us, acting on some instinct, find a bad mirror that restores the child we used to be? I started to think of this behavior as mundane masochism, so ordinary it avoids detection. A poet in Cambridge, Massachusetts, hearing me discussing this one day, exclaimed that after her day's writing, she always opened *The New Yorker*, read its poems, and told herself: "See? That's why you're unpublished." Still, others, I knew, rushed to share fresh work with someone ready to organize and straighten and slash but unable to enter into the messy inner life of the thing.

Mundane masochism isn't limited to our writing life, of course. We transform ourselves back to our "before" state in myriad ways even though we belong to a culture that worships the rags-to-riches story, the kid savant with a cyberbusiness that's now worth a billion, the drugstore beauty who's "discovered." Sometimes the bad mirror in which we find our old self is a partner who is emotionally inaccessible; he summons that old childhood hurt. Sometimes the mirror is a lover who is sad the way one's parent was sad. You can shovel your whole life into cheering him, but his unhappiness always belongs to him; you can't take it away. You can only jig faster, grin wider.

And writing requires departure. You are leaving your accustomed companions. Will you still be safe? Will you be allowed to return? The piece is getting exciting and peculiar. Will you let the scissor flash of pigeon wings carry you up into a vision that may be oracular, might be ridiculous?

In the first fiction-writing class I ever took, the novelist Gilbert Sorrentino told about a talented man whose writing he encouraged. This man stopped writing. Sorrentino spoke about it bitterly, as if he'd been betrayed, as if it had cost him something terrible to give encouragement. I wondered what wild, rare gifts this man had possessed. Sorrentino also said, "Reality is a railroad train and some of us are tied to the tracks." Was the gifted man the tied-down person? Or was the person Sorrentino, who stalked into class glowering in a leather jacket, camouflage trousers and a dark-blue beret? And was it his gifts that tied him down? I didn't know what to make of Sorrentino's remark and I didn't know why he was bitter, and I didn't understand why students kept hemorrhaging from the class until, although a hundred students had started out in the giant lecture hall at the New School, by the last week only about eighteen students remained. All I knew was that I wanted to write.

I lived with my parents in the Bronx. My sister read a book called *Life Is with People*. I thought the title got it wrong. Life is with books, it's with ideas. It hadn't occurred to me that life experiences might, in themselves, be worthwhile. I was working at the Guinness Book of World Records, and all day long people would call up wanting to know if they could finally get into the book. "Stop eating salamanders!" I'd hear a clerk down the hall declare. "It's not a category." "Cut your toenails. You won't get in." You could only enter the book if you'd broken a record in an established field, if the regulations for your achievement already existed. Still the phone rang with people who'd skipped the book's rules, they were so desperate to enter.

After work, on Monday nights, I walked from my job at Twenty-Seventh Street to Twelfth Street. There, before class at The New School, I scarfed a slice of pizza at Famous Ray's—my sister Anita had praised this restaurant, and so it had a kind of authoritative glamour I associated with her, despite the grunginess of its digs. This was the original Famous Ray's, she'd told me, unless a certain different joint was. There were Famous Ray's all over the city, which magnified the mystery of the true identity. Was I in the right place? Before class I sat eating the crackling, tender dough, and gazed at the orange oil pool on the plate where the glassine paper was going translucent, and hoped that the class would give me lessons in how to write. After class I took the subway to the second-to-last stop at the very end of the line in the Bronx, and then waited for a city bus. I registered most emphatically the incidental stories that the teacher told but only in retrospect, several years later, could I discern his acid tone and recall, with a belated spark of realization, that one student—an older, and canny man— complained pointedly about our teacher's nastiness.

Which is to say, I had little sense of reality. I didn't recognize the railroad and I didn't recognize the railroad tracks. My good fortune was that all I really wanted was to be a writer. By this I meant to be someone for whom stories unspooled, who could call forth the glimmering, quicksilver song of things. I imagined such a person—a real writer—would be possessed of an inalienable inner assurance. Years later when I saw a photo of Louise Erdrich with her arms crossed in a posture of serene, bemused confidence and wearing dangling silver-and-turquoise earrings, I thought, "Yes. That." And when I saw a photo of Amy Tan in a squared Chinese silk toque, I thought, "Exactly." It was a shamanistic, placid arrogation of the role of the storyteller. Both women were older sisters who had enjoyed a certain stature in their families.

At my own family table, I ate hastily and wandered away. If I did tell a story about my day, whatever I said contracted down to a sentence or two, its importance dwindling as I spoke. And yet I knew that this was a misperception. The things I'd witnessed possessed vital force. The world with its brittle green polynoses under the oak tree, and its earthworms that manifested themselves on the pavement after rain, and the white glass stars on an especially cold Bronx night—there must be a way to convey these.

Only later did I realize that my stories shrank because my parents didn't have the emotional wealth at the time to be able to pay attention. The discrete objects of this world, however, continued to shine their beauty up at me: The iridescent green-and-yellow dragon scales that stood in my palm after I peeled an orange. The mermaids on the bathroom wallpaper with tails curled like tridents—each object like what Freud means when he talks about a screen memory.

A screen memory is a memory in which extra information has been stored. Freud likens its texture to that of a brocaded quilt—here is this extra lumpiness, this added swell of emotion, a sudden sense of mysterious affective importance surging into what ought to be, judging from the facts of the event, something dull and flat. A screen memory hides emotional truths that belong elsewhere. My world remained a diaspora world, significance swollen and pulsing and scattered. And I longed for the day I would be able to transmit the dots and dashes of this life and hear its meaning.

I longed to write or at least discover a volume in whose pages I would find the significance of each coded object—those shimmering translucent fish scales in my palm, the oak keys which Anita had pointed out and thus seemed to invent, the smashed glass in the night sky over the schoolyard of J.H.S. 82 where this same sister Anita rode on a creaking, wide-wheeled one-speed bike, laughing like a maniac, me on the handlebars, the wind in our faces like life flinging itself at us. I craved to be a poet who could sing the significance of that shattered world, a talker who, like Anita, conjured each thing she named.

My wish came true in Boston, where I wrote on a novel in the morning. Oh, the violence of craving a transformation! The tricky power of the thing! "When the effort for change heats up the psyche," writes Robert Bly, "the heat itself attracts demons, or sleeping complexes, or bitter enemies of the spirit.... The invader might be chaos, but the enemy also feels as if it were part of our own soul." Dismay with the old life propels the yearning for a change, but there's a catch. The old life was you. How can you feel you are yourself when you leave yourself behind?

We would rather feel real than feel good, some of us. We'd rather feel authentic than thrilled. When the Hawaii book no longer evoked envy, I searched for a different book—impatient, urgent, flinging aside volume after volume. There was a kind of blankness—an achy surcease of feeling—that I yearned for as I tossed aside pages, searching for glittering prose against which I could gash myself. Ascetic or lyrical, minimalist or capacious, it didn't matter; any excellence sufficed. Once I found it, I slowed way down. I read with care. Then, numb, I walked through the airless Prudential plaza and out into the city.

Now I could sit all afternoon in the Mutual of New York Life Insurance Company office, sipping a 24-ounce wax jug of iced coffee from Dunkin' Donuts, answering Mr. Kameras's telephone, filing Mr. Kameras's premium-payment receipts, gazing through the plank of sealed-shut window in early spring as the sapling in its square of pavement whipped about, lashing the air.

Easier at that time of my life to occupy a dissociated world than to insist on the pattern of things as I saw them. Easier to smash the constellations apart again than let my pictures cohere. Because my perceptions had their flaws, I knew. And someone in the outside world might, gloatingly, point them out. Viewed from a different angle, after all, everything I saw might be something else. My mother was actually powerful, my sister Anita was actually weak and kind, my younger brother Ken tyrannical, my other brother nurturing, and my father was, in his own way, ruthless. What I thought was right-side up might be upside down. I did not yet realize that one can—that one must—advocate for the value of one's work and vision. It wasn't being Mr. Kameras's secretary that bothered me. I liked answering the phones; I liked typing. They were soothing, familiar activities. What I didn't like was being returned to feeling like a dull-witted girl. That is: I didn't like being the "before," although it was I who'd restored her.

I excised my excitement, afraid I saw the world through a lens of distortion, then gazed out the sealed window of my glassed-in office at the lone sapling furiously smashing at everything near.

In fact, I was sure my excitement damaged things. So of course it needed to be sequestered. One day when I was a child my mother finished knitting a red cable-knit cardigan and held it up. It was my size! She had been making it for me. It had taken her month upon month. I was very familiar with that bag of crimson wool with the two pearly blue sleek needles sticking out. Now she held up the finally finished garment—a beautiful raspberry cable knit—and called me over. I loved it, and felt almost awed with gratitude. She had been thinking of me the entire time she made it! I wasn't invisible to her! She buttoned me into it, although it was still summer—high August—and, exultant, off I set. But that very first afternoon, running, I tumbled down into a thicket and the wool became embedded with briars. Nettles the size of chiggers tore the fabric when I pulled them out but scratched my skin if I left them embedded. My mother was horrified. She nearly wept when she saw. Precious things shouldn't be entrusted to me. My mother herself found my eager hands an attack, an imposition, as if she were a sweater I was painfully embedded in; she flinched, and plucked my hands away.

Growing up, I associated excitement with destruction, pleasure with damage. So, I saved up the dangerous joy of writing by destroying it. I'd have it again tomorrow, at my desk. In the meantime, I'd be Insurance Office Girl, zonked, secure, my secret identity stored away inside me. I was a walking screen memory: dull on the surface, yet swollen with something I couldn't name.

My Clark Kent self stepped out of the bookstore, drifted blearily toward the T. She wore a starched blouse, greenish circle skirt, and heels so worn on the bricks of Government Plaza that the toes curled like Arabic lamps; the true me stayed home at the desk.

We absorb everything that happens to us. We ingest it. The swaggering, sardonic teacher. The creaking bike. The sweater that is too good for us and the scratchy briars that swarm through it. The mother on her lawn chair, clacking the needles that produce the cable knit. The father with a switchblade mouth under kind, wet eyes. Each of us who does so has our own idiosyncratic reason for changing ourselves back to who we were before—and yet, echoing through them all is a common reason. We do not believe we deserve to feel better.

"Do you always go into the bookstore?" asked a friend.

"Yes! It's very informative!"

"You always do this?"

"Yes!"

"But don't you find that interesting?"

I didn't. And then suddenly I did.

And then it became possible to quit. Once I began to see how I was searching for myself in bad mirrors, it could stop, although in the beginning I had to force my feet to walk past the bookstore and not go in. Over time I became oblivious of the bookstore. New patterns set in. I let *The New Yorker* wait in the mailbox until evening rather than reading it the hour it arrived with its news of who had achieved success. And I stopped sharing my most exciting ideas with people who returned them to me as if they'd been through a hot dryer: shrunken, toy-sized, almost ludicrous versions of their former selves.

I had to cut the cycle of reversion. I had to accept that the cockeyed ungainly clutch purse that I'd knitted was in its own provisional way okay. It wasn't Anita's evenly stitched afghan, or my mother's exquisite cardinal-red sweater, but it was something, with its mother-of-pearl oculus button, its yellow-wheat hue, its lining that my mother had sewn in, its hatchet shape, its memory of stitches appearing that had been conjured by my own fingers, a texture accumulating. It was a start.

I had to surrender my hunger for a transformation. I had to give up my desire to be other than I was. I had to recant the old idolatries, leave off the mermaid in-between state, half-fish, half-woman, and accept my own reality as I perceived it, and to accept as well the scenes that kept rising through the soil like earthworms after a rain. One cannot be an artist and prefer pristine unknowing innocence, the atomized, blurred perspective, the stepping back into the amniotic ball of oblivion. One must allow one's view to cohere.

I had to allow the definitive. I had to allow clarity. To leave the stupor fog, the ingenue's unknowing.

Envy, I discovered, is self-estrangement. It is using another person to empty you of yourself. Every day there can be someone else to envy. The TV flashes their images; the newspaper spreads them before you in black and white. It always seems as if the envied person is doing something to us, is evoking our envy and scooping us out, but of course there is no other person. There is only ink on wood pulp, pixels on glass, this limited amount of information about a real person whose particular human unhappiness, should we ever discover it, surprises. How dare they be unhappy when they are so rich, when they have taken so much from us? What did they take? Our ability to enjoy our own particular life. An envied person, I've come to learn, blinds us to the beauty our own life already reveals.

These days I tell my students what I've learned: The antidote to self-sabotage is to reconnect with the beauty your work and your life already possess. When you reject who you are, you stoke the cycle of reversion. Your experiences, your way of sharing them— their value is infinite. On your own passage into the city of men and women, don't break faith with your vision.The beauty you seek is stowed away abundantly in your own thistles and seedpods, your own mermaids and Sorrentinos, your own crooked and shattered and Buddha friends, your own mad rides on creaky bikes under the shimmering heavens, the whole whirling journey of the thing, your sister's glorious laughter in your ear, telling you, for all its wildness, as if it was the breath of life itself, which it was, yes, yes, darling, yes. Let yourself be carried away. And, after, refuse humiliation.

MY GERTRUDE STEIN

Anita slept three feet away. From across the ocean between us she described the glories she witnessed. She could look straight into the apartments across the street.

She saw an unmade bed, a man and a woman drinking out of cocktail glasses in a tiny gold kitchen, a cat poised in the window like a vase, and a woman in a poufy plastic shower cap pulling on pantyhose and then throwing perfume between her legs. Anita narrated. I saw just a corner of cabinet and a piece of distant wall. Once I saw a door shut, but I could never see who shut it, even though I stared until even in my dreams I was seeing that shut door. From my view, everything across the street seemed molded of dust, inconsequential. If only I had Anita's bed!

"Star position's what I call this," she said. "It's how to sleep when the weather's hot."

Arms splayed, legs far as they'd divide, she looked voluminous, voluptuous.

Beyond her, the door to the terrace hung open on its chain. It was a humid night. The streetlight held a dusty smudge around it, an agglutination of air as if we were breathing chalk. Anita sighed. "What a breeze," she murmured.

"I didn't feel anything."

"No? There, that. Did you feel that?"

"No." I twisted in my sheets.

"Wait," she said. "Okay, now nothing. Nothing. Now there. It's—oh. It's exquisite. Like a cat brushing past. Like, like—no, now it's over."

"But I didn't feel anything," I moaned.

She stretched, more starlike.

"Let me have your bed. Just one night," I said.

"You chose your bed."

"Ages ago!"

"So what?"

When we first moved to Riverdale, the street had frightened me. In our old apartment the windows were far away, and a big blue tree guarded us like a risen moon. Here the city pressed close. The streetlight was an inquisition, and people walked under our window, jangling the change in their pockets. I wanted to be toward the room's inside, toward the hallways, the narrow ventricles winding to my parents. I'd begged Anita to take that bed.

But now beside the open door I imagined she heard the tidal music of the street. I heard it too, but like the ocean in a shell: miniaturized. She heard the real thing, car whoosh, laughter, the far-off haul of the 100 bus curving around the Henry Hudson Parkway, and the whispery road itself, an asphalt arrow pointing away. Anita's whole body pointed away, legs, arms, and even stomach, which rose to meet the world, and which had lots of the world inside it. She ate what she pleased. Jelly donuts, Godiva chocolates, tender slabs of farmer cheese, lavender wafers that tasted like soap, that tasted like churches, and which came in a beautiful package, all silver and purple. Anita was like an iguana or a baby, learning the world through her mouth. She advanced one tongue's length at a time. By now she was deep into Manhattan shops and mail-order catalogues, which she read with biblical attention, staring at the pictures in Lillian Vernon, ordering the stamp-thin ginger crisps, the Jordan almonds colored like sun-bleached gum balls and just as hard, the Danish cookies that crumbled to sugar at the first bite, spending her babysitting money with a wild hand.

I imagined grand futures for Anita. She had the aura of someone on TV. She spoke in such capacious sentences, with so many passionately expressed opinions and odd facts built in, that while she spoke I felt undeserving. Others should hear her. She should be a personality like Julia Child. She could tell the plot of a *Mannix* episode in more time than it took to watch it and yet she kept it interesting. She could describe what she'd seen on the street so that you felt you'd seen it, too. Above her flame-blue eyes, her bangs lay straight as a level. Anita cut them herself. But she let her ponytail bush out in a thicket behind her, as if what was over her shoulder did not exist. It was a snare, a rat's nest, a clotted glory. My grandmother threatened to snip it off; my mother whispered in a loud and mournful voice what a shame it was that such a pretty girl should have such an unruly head. Anita smiled. She sat in an orange flower-power muumuu sipping Swee-Touch-Nee and eating candied fruit slices with my friends' mothers, and giving her opinion about a daughter who ran off to get married or a son who needed the name of an excellent dermatologist. She was fifteen. It was just a matter of time before she lived beside the Seine.

Yet for all Anita's aplomb and appetite, I told the therapist I began to see in my early thirties, it was I who left. I went off—I realized now—to find a place where I didn't covet someone else's bed or chair, where I was who I wanted to be. In fact, I wanted to be Anita. The real Anita stayed in the Bronx. She stayed more and more in her body. Her arms weakened; her legs stiffened into marble sculpture that she needed to be balanced over, or she'd collapse.

How to match the girls we were to the women we became? A sister's life interrogates yours, saying Why do you live this way? Are you doing what's right? And when the sister has a disease, I discovered, she has it for you, so you don't have to have it, just the way she picked up heavy knapsacks when she was stronger than you, or took the bed beneath the windows when you begged, so you could feel safe.

"I weigh as much as the street Yankee Stadium is on," she told me from the hospital to which she'd recently moved. This was the hospital in the movie *Awakenings*, and there were yellowed clippings on many patients' walls showing Robin Williams here. Anita's roommate, Kathleen, was an extra. Kathleen has cerebral palsy, and a sign taped to the back of her chair: "Leave me the hell alone" below a picture of Edvard Munch's *The Scream*.

"As much as the street Yankee Stadium is on?" I said. "How much is that?"

"One hundred sixty-eight."

"Oh."

"And now they're going to put Yankee Stadium in New Jersey. I think it's a shame. The Bronx has so many problems right now, it needs Yankee Stadium. Besides, what would Yankee Stadium do in New Jersey? It wouldn't be the same thing at all. It would be meaningless."

"You're right," I said. Anita came to Beth Abraham when she could hardly walk, and every day she was more static, while I kept traveling further and further from home.

"I hear you're going on vacation to Mexico," she said. "Send me a postcard."

"Okay. Hey, do you remember the postcard you sent me from Israel? It was an airplane, Anita! A Pan Am jet."

"I call that a good postcard," she responded. "You wanted to see travel, and travel is what I sent."

"Oooh, you're a smart one!"

"Jane Lilly is always telling me to join Mensa," she said. "She thinks I'm wasting myself."

"You are not wasting yourself. You are providing wonderful conversation to everyone around you."

"I'm glad you think so," she said.

I did.

When I began psychoanalysis, Anita was the one topic I refused to talk about. I'd begun a novel about her, and I was afraid if I told my story I wouldn't need to write it.

"Have you had the experience of things you shared being appropriated?" Harriet asked.

"No."

"You haven't had the experience of things you told about being taken away?"

"Not in particular."

Occasionally Harriet's chin looked fleshy and stubborn, like Anita's. Occasionally I heard the ball of her palm rubbing callously against the page as she took notes. This reminded me of Anita, too: an insensitive body pursuing its own course.

"Your body sometimes seems really clumsy to me," I said dreamily, from my position on the couch.

"Does it?"

"Yes." But I was momentarily distracted by her computer with its screen saver of an oblong folding in on itself, turning into a triangle, then pivoting to reveal a new dimension which made it oblong again. I ventured: "I was thinking of how you always say that I envy you, but maybe you envy me."

"And what would I envy?"

"That I get to lie here and tell you all the stories I see and think."

"Would you like me to envy you?"

"No!"

"But the way you know you have something good is when you worry about someone else's envy."

I considered this, then said: "Smart." The screen saver spawned another angle.

"You've been thinking about Anita," said Harriet.

"Yes."

"You often are when you think about my clumsy body."

I crossed my arms. "I still don't like to talk about her with you."

"Even though you've had so many fights with friends?"

I nodded. "Actually, I was just remembering a time I think Anita did appropriate—to use a word of yours—something of mine. I was lying on the bedroom floor and trying to fix a crooked stamp hinge onto the back of a stamp, and Anita came in and stood over me and made some observation. She pointed out that I was using a stapled-together album, and she'd also started with that years ago, but now she'd graduated to the great big double-volume loose-leaf album. I think she meant to be encouraging. But the second she left, I just squeezed and squeezed that boring, stupid-seeming little stamp into a smithereen and threw it under my bed."

Harriet scratched in her notebook.

"Sometimes you remind me of Anita," I said. "You try to encourage, but it has the opposite effect. Sometimes you seem very bossy—"

I stopped.

"Yes?"

"Anita wasn't bossy. I don't know why I said that."

"She wasn't bossy?"

I shook my head. "No. She was good. I loved her."

Harriet was silent.

"Things change, around you. There's a loving way to see and there's a different way. A cold way. The way we see things here seems—unloving."

"Is it unloving to see the truth?"

"Anita doesn't deserve to be seen in any but the most loving way."

"I'm not suggesting anything else."

"No, of course not! How could I even imagine otherwise?"

She set down her notebook. "You're angry," she observed.

"I don't want any more transformations of how I feel about people."

She nodded her suddenly pudgy-chinned face.

Anita sewed little books. Palm-sized, they were cheap typing paper stitched with three bold strokes. Into these books she set fabulous stories about sisters and fireworks and pounding drums. You opened the book and stepped in.

I copied her books and called them mine. "By Bonita Friedman," I wrote. I folded the same kind of paper, then sewed it the way Anita taught, with a long needle that hurt my thumb when I shoved it through the wadded sheets. I drew the fireworks she drew, and the two sisters walking, their hands like five-pronged forks entwined, their skirts like little bells, and their hair a flip. Crayon smell filled the room, or else the besotting scent of markers—you had to use orange with such care: it soaked everything.

Some days Anita drew her stories on spools of adding-machine paper she bought for thirty-five cents at the Temple bazaar. Those days I drew scrolls too, persuaded by watching Anita that really these were better than books, these tales taped to a pencil at one end and rolling around and around, girls following fireworks following pigeons and alley cats and cocktail glasses and drums and more girls still holding hands until they all lived in a realm you could enter anywhere, a great big bolster like a thicker and thicker epithelium made of a tissue of stories.

In fact, lacking adding-machine paper, we sometimes used toilet paper, which required an agony of tenderness and much precise administering of that orange, which bled like Merthiolate. The result was a sort of saturated snowball of color that to the uninitiated might look like a collapsed mess, but which, to Anita and me, was visual shorthand for stories themselves. Once finished, the tissue scrolls were too fragile to open: they nested like eggs in Anita's drawer. Glimpsing one imparted an instant's delirium, my first contact high.

While we worked, Anita sat on the scabby yellow Windsor chair. I sat at her elbow on an overturned wastebasket that pictured Bohack-brand vegetables. Where did Anita's stories come from? I wondered. How did she know how to draw? Somehow she saw that fireworks were airborne spiders, and that curtains hung in windows like a central part in a chunky girl's hair. She had a visual alphabet that encompassed a million things: garbage pails were webbed tubes, flowerpots were cups with a cuff out of which poked a circular serrated flower, hats were flying saucers squashed on round heads, money was an oblong with a dollar sign in someone's hand. Anything you asked, Anita could draw in this simplified, charming way.

Similarly, her handwriting, always print, was unstoppably expressive, a parade of characters tumbling across the page, her plump lowercase *a* reminiscent of the corpulent Winston Churchill propped by a cane, her *m* the top of the Ten Commandments. I watched the letters appear out the tip of her pen. What fun to be her, I imagined. Collections assembled around her. In her big white Formica desk stood sky-blue letters from pen pals, each marked "Answered," pamphlets from Weight Watchers shaped like loan coupon books, wool "God's eyes," gold-plated charms for a charm bracelet. There was even an envelope of phosphorescent pollen. This was shimmery yellow green, an exhalation of the trees, which Anita had swept from a country porch at our sleepaway camp. I'd seen Anita's heels glowing like night-lights. "Anita!" I'd said. She looked and laughed. "Pine tree pollen," she announced, and swept it up in one of the little envelopes she carried in her pocket as nature counselor.

That envelope now lay in a coil, bound by a rubber band, in her top drawer. I seldom saw it. Anita rarely granted permission to look in her desk. A feminine scent of bath powder sifted up when you opened a drawer, and I once discovered a fascinating lumpy package that looked like it should unfold but wouldn't: a sanitary napkin, Anita later explained.

I knew the inside of Anita was like the inside of all these things, of the desk, the books. The inside of her was like the sky on Independence Day, lit with the fireworks she loved, or the black crayoned drawings she taught me to scratch with a pin, revealing rainbows of nighttime carnival underneath. She was the first person I met who had an actual internal life. How I wished I were she!

What is it to grow up wanting someone else's eyes and fingers and mouth and mind? I erased so much of what I wrote in second grade, my teacher cracked the tops off my pencils. At home, I sat very close to Anita. I thought if I copied her long enough, I would learn how to create.

Anita seemed to copy no one. She went off to Israel, and came back with a tingle in her elbow that wouldn't go away. This tingle was the beginning of her body erasing herself, the myelin sheaths around her nerve endings degrading, forming obdurate scar tissue—although this took a while to find out. I was there the day the doctor stuck a needle in Anita's palm and she felt nothing. I saw the needle jab, and Anita, with her eyes closed, waiting for a feeling to start.

"Anything now?" asked the doctor.

"No. Not yet," Anita said.

The doctor pushed the needle against another part of her hand. "And now?"

"I don't feel a thing. Are you touching me? I don't feel anything. I can't feel a thing."

I also saw Anita, with her eyes closed and her arms out, attempt to walk straight across the examining room. She took one baby step and then another, and the more she walked, the more she diverged.

"Anita," I said, and she opened her eyes.

She was in the wrong part of the room.

"Here is your pocketbook," I said. "I want to go home."

After that, in the mornings as we rode the #1 subway together to our jobs, Anita read brochures she'd sent away for, slowly turning the pages. Laetrile therapies, Swiss spa therapies, thermal therapies. "I wish I had the money for this," said Anita, tapping a page. I looked. A clinic in Mexico that cost thousands for a drug treatment involving SAM-e.

"Oh, it's bogus!" I said. "It makes me so angry. They're just trying to prey on your fears." I was afraid to say "hopes."

"There might be something to it."

I shook my head and looked away. "I really doubt it."

"But maybe there is." She tucked the brochures back into her satchel.

"They say if it begins mildly, it will continue mildly," I said.

She took my hand in her small one, and the train rocked as we flew into the darkness after Dykeman Street. How hot her palm was! Did she have a fever?

"It began mildly," I muttered. We got off at the same stop on the subway—Thirty-Fourth Street—and she walked briskly beside me in pressed trousers and a cranberry wool coat. At the door of her office building she hugged me hard, and I ran the rest of the way to my own building.

* * *

Where Anita lives now, men and women loll in wheelchairs. Pieces of them are missing. Some have a bandaged stump where a leg should be. Others are too skinny, and remain collapsed sideways in their wheelchairs. Their eyes follow you down the linoleum, past the cafe where angels—volunteers—serve weak coffee and day-old chocolate chip cookies, and where many wheelchairs are lined up in late autumn, so that people can gaze out at the treeless courtyard, the peeling white gazebo, the two patchy street cats, black and white, climbing the wood like squirrels, and then dashing across the pavement. "Look! Look at that cat! She's so fast!" a patient murmurs admiringly.

People here are friendly. If you ask one patient where the elevator is, three or four answer. They all point you down the hallway, elaborate what you will pass on the way, and, like parents, watch your progress. To each other they don't say much, though. That's the way with people together from dusk to dawn.

The home has a compelling, miraculous atmosphere. The heat is amniotic. You're on the verge of a sweat. An antiseptic fatigue enfolds you. The sand in an hourglass is floating up and down throughout the corridors. Time has assumed a gauzy detachment, a free-floating deep-space granular air—as if a field of dandelion seeds are drifting, as if all the Jean Naté Anita ever powdered is invisibly rising in a gust and subsiding again. "Doctor Hall, report to the third floor, please. Security, pick up line two." Even in the bathrooms, broadcasts permeate. No doors matter. Nurses and TVs and PA systems can enter even one's dreams.

During Anita's birthday party her new roommate, Rhea, left her TV tuned to Sunday afternoon football, although she didn't watch. A woman in her late seventies, Rhea sat in a pink robe and slippers, an old *Newsweek* lying in her lap. "Thank you, darling," she said when I gave her a piece of cake, and "No thank you, darling," when I offered coffee. Mostly, she daydreamed. Meanwhile, the rapid, monotone male voice on the set announced plays, cheers erupted like static, and there were flickering shots of bent men running, charging, posing themselves in configuration. We licked our frosting and Anita opened her cards bathed by the sportscaster's excited, distant voice.

When my phone rings at home, and the stranger at the other end firmly advises what to add to my guacamole or what's coming up on *Entertainment Tonight*, I know it's Anita. "And now the latest on the president's summit trip," I hear, and she materializes in the foreground: "Bon? How are you?" She seems to be reporting live from the scene, stealing a private moment. Still, the loud impersonality of the voices behind her imparts a sense of futility, as if she's calling from a loveless place.

Anita asks me to take home Mishka, the Olympic teddy bear. She didn't ask me to bring him, she says, and wishes I hadn't. This is a hospital, and ought to look like one. She's leaving as soon as she's strong enough, she says. Twice a week she has physical therapy.

Twice a week seems very little to me, almost a token amount. But, wouldn't it be wonderful if she could get stronger? Who's to say it won't happen? Who's to say it out loud? Maybe a miracle will happen. Maybe a doctor will discover how to make nerves grow back.

"I'll take Mishka next time I come," I say.

"Good. I want him home, next to the piano. And take home the poster of orange groves, too. The more you bring now, the less we'll have to occupy our arms with later."

"You don't want it there to cheer you up?"

"It does not cheer me up to have it here."

When the elevator door opens on the sixth floor of Beth Abraham, I usually find Anita sitting outside her bedroom door. She wears cherry-red or navy-blue cotton housedresses with snaps down the front, which my mother buys at Kress's. She reads *Ellery*

Queen's Mystery Magazine, holding the pages close.

"Let's get your coat," I announce.

"Bonnie!"

"Where's your hat? Do you want your purse?"

"I had no idea you were coming today! I want a kiss." She tilts her face to the side, and I kiss her.

"Now, where's your other glove?" I say. "I've sprung you! I've signed you out. Let's get some fresh air."

"Slow down!"

"Oh, it's not cold out. You don't need your other glove. Let's go."

Nothing feels as good as getting Anita out of here.

I don't like what's happened in therapy. I feel as if I'm scraping the bottom of the pot, as if a pot of milky coffee got scalded, and when I scrape, a big brown piece floats up. I pluck it out and chew on it. Bitterness fills my mouth. I feel increasingly estranged from my husband and parents, and even from my own self. Paper has been inserted between the layers of me. I feel detached, deadened, and anxious.

"You always felt detached and deadened," Harriet claims. "These are your earliest experiences."

"I miss joy," I say. "I used to feel joy."

"You are taking your happiness away from your own self. Don't you see? It's intrapsychic."

I laugh. "Paul says, 'Intrapsychic's just another way of saying, It's in yo' own head!'"

"I miss my old view of Anita," I add. I used to think of Anita with wild affection and pity. She was overweight in adolescence, and I recall watching from the bedroom window as she toiled up the street in her oatmeal cloth coat, moving like a fifty-year-old woman although she was seventeen. How that sight contracted my heart!

Now, though, my view of her has flattened. Was she domineering, or is this simply a puny, resentful, younger-sister way of seeing her? I can perceive her as either magical or mean. When I feel she was mean, I hate her, and have no access to her magic; the world drains of color. When I see her as magical, gratitude floods me. I love you, Anita, I want to proclaim. Yet at those moments some part of me is left out. Some part of me is banished into the hall. And the part of me hugging Anita feels hollow, ersatz.

"*You* are now the magical one," I observe.

I fall silent but her pen keeps scratching, long past how much I've said. For an instant I imagine it is the act of taking notes behind my back that has given the therapist such disproportionate power. She has burrowed her way into me. What is she writing?

"What's in that white bowl?" I point to her Matisse print. "It looks like it's either arsenic or milk."

"Which do you think it is?"

"Well, poison. Unless it's milk. It's like you. Sometimes you seem extremely beautiful, and the thought of you fills me with good feelings. Other times, though, I feel like you're cruel and greedy, and using me for your own purposes. But then I look over and see you, and I'm ashamed of my thoughts. I can't stand all the distortions."

"The distortions are transference. They're a sign that the therapy is working."

"The difference between us is that you think the distortions accurately portray what's inside me."

"And you?"

"I think they're distortions!"

"There must have been other people in your life before me about whom you felt ambivalent, who you felt oppressed by and yet loved."

I smile. "I'd like to know the truth about you," I say.

"Ah."

The truth of something lurks in its proxy, I know by now. Anita, I occasionally even see, is a proxy for me. She was the angry, bullying daughter I wasn't. "I wish I could release Anita, free her from her rigid body. Get her walking again. And I would like to crack open my own rigid sense of her and let the love out. I can't feel it." After a moment I add, "When I was a child, I used to tell Anita, 'I can't feel anything from here!'" The black chickens in the Matisse print seem extremely static, bonnets in a row.

"Why couldn't you feel anything?"

"I was too far from the door to the terrace at night. Anita felt the most ineffable breezes, I believed—breezes that seemed more wonderful than any I'd ever felt. You know, Harriet," I said abruptly, shaking my head in frustration, "I sometimes feel as if you've broken into me. I have a friend who says whenever she falls in love she dreams of a house broken into. I feel invaded. I wish I could terminate this therapy. But I'm afraid I'd be lost without it, that I'd be unable to do my work. I've become dependent on you."

"Maybe you've never been close to someone who would tolerate your desire to leave. You had to stay and do what the other wanted in order to feel safe. But you felt rigid."

I laugh. "Yes! You're absolutely right! Keep talking! When you were speaking I felt—oh, such joy! Such wild joy!"

We are silent. I am trying to savor the moment. The sun flings a golden carpet across the floor. It swirls with dust, like a sparkling scrim curtain rising. For an instant my cheek is cooled by a delicious breeze, and I'm sure she feels it.

Anita fell, and I became the star. What sort of joy can there be in this? My handwriting looks like what hers used to. Her handwriting looks like a child's now. I found her once in the hospital's empty dining room, writing a postcard against the paper tablecloth. She was writing to Jane Lilly, her friend who lived in Reno, Nevada. Nine or ten of her arduously shaped words would fit on the whole card. She laid her pen down in midsentence. It took so long to write each word, she would finish the card later.

Just going to the bathroom is an expedition now. Anita has become mindful of small pleasures. "Mom brought me a basket of strawberries and two cans of Coca-Cola when she came yesterday," she tells me. "When I'm done drinking them, I'll rinse out the cans and save them for Mark." Anita had suspected an orderly had taken some of her cans. Now she keeps them locked in her cabinet.

"Her horizons have narrowed to a pinpoint," my mother once said.

Mine have expanded. I have a bed by the road, a night view of stories. The black field of my computer screen kindles with tangerine letters, like the art Anita taught me, black crayon scratched to rainbows underneath. But these glories don't feel entirely mine. I'd wanted to become Anita, but I'm me, sitting in her place. How can I help but feel fraudulent? In her sleep, Anita can still walk. In my sleep, I'm still on the Bohack garbage can.

"My body is attacking itself," Anita said over the phone recently.

I nodded, twisting the cord between my fingers.

"When people ask me how come you're here," she said, "I tell them, 'Because I donated my blood to the floor.' The first time was on my birthday. The insurance company came, picked me up, and took me to the E.R. They stitched up this part of my head so the blood would stop. After the second time, I was brought here. Two days ago I saw the neurologist. He said, 'I haven't seen you in a year.' 'You haven't cured me in a year, either,' I told him. We talked. What doctors generally do is ask questions. You give them answers."

"I've noticed that, too," I said.

"Well, there are a lot of things they still don't know. Speaking of which, did I tell you there's a man here that wants to feel me up? I told him, no. You are my boyfriend but Mark is my husband."

"Anita, don't let him! Unless you want him to."

"I don't want him to. But, you know, we all get old at the same rate. One day at a time."

"Meaning?"

"I'm happy for the attention, I suppose."

Once upon a time I wanted Anita's attention. I craved to see the world from her perspective. When she went to Israel after college, all her furniture became mine. The bed had a trough. The desk was stuffy. Steam pumped from behind it in a way that gave me a headache. I studied into the night. Sometimes a motion reflected in the night glass jolted me. Was the door opening? Was it Anita come back early?

I sat for hours on my ankles, bending my head beneath the halo of her Lightolier lamp, desperate to forge a mind. I felt as if I was pushing books into my head. I wanted to shove a whole library in my head, and was disappointed by my memory. Certain facts I'd known in October had vanished by April. I had to put them back in again. Summer came, and I spent it exiled among pine trees at a sleepaway camp. I sat on a big rock and ate fizzy candy and fake-vanilla ice cream bars bought from the canteen, and by September my head was empty again. I gazed at the apartments across the street. They still seemed uninhabited.

Anita, meanwhile, was walking in orange groves, sipping ginger in her coffee, cutting purple cabbage into salads heaped with fresh feta cheese she served her new friends, speaking Hebrew at the ulpan and practicing Italian to sing arias at the Rubin Academy. She wrote home on the translucent blue paper I'd always admired, the paper that was a layer of sky you could hold in your hand. Anita plucked some sky, covered it with her adventures, and sealed it all around with a lick of her tongue. The return address was in hiero-glyphs more expressive than anything I'd ever imagined. Her bet was a serene dove, gazing. Her aleph an upright person who could also bend. "Answered," I wrote on her envelope before tucking it in her drawer. Whatever spot I occupied, I wasn't in the desirable place.

"You feel guilty because your secret wish for Anita came true. You must have wanted her to fall, as a girl."

"That sounds very intelligent," I say, "but I have no memory of that."

Although suddenly I recall sitting beside her in my father's LeSabre and noticing how my two yellowish bare legs pressed together made one of hers. Surely there was mockery in that? I'd gazed at my own fleshy thighs and saw how much fatter hers were—and wasn't that my way of expressing my dislike of her for commanding so much of my father's attention?

"Sometimes I have a funny urge, Harriet, to actually push you out of that chair! And yet I want you in it."

"My equanimity seems like an insult to you."

I smile. "Yes! And there's a way your interpretations keep you far away from me, holding you at a kind of exalted distance. Here I'm so messy and needy while you're so composed. It reminds me of how Anita was always associated in my mind with calluses, some-thing obdurate and fleshy. But," I say with a sigh, "I now appreciate that her detached manner was just her way of protecting herself. You want to hear something odd? Paul and I came across some pictures of Anita recently from when she was at Music and Art High School. She wasn't fat. That was just the family myth. She was maybe fifteen pounds overweight, if that. She was actually very pretty and a little voluptuous. But she wasn't fat. She put on weight later, at college. But I wonder where the family idea that she was a fat girl came from? It was something we all just simply agreed about."

Harriet nodded.

In one of the photos I'd found, Anita sat in a tangerine triangular paper hat and blue sweater, at the Chinese pavilion at the World's Fair, delicately sipping what looked like iced tea. She'd been sixteen. She wore rose lipstick and her hair was neatly brushed back, and her snug sweater showed her elegant, womanly body. I'd recalled when the photo was first developed and my father saw it. He said: "You look so attractive in this picture, Anita." And she did, with a mature elegance and vulnerability that I envied.

"Maybe she seemed fat because she wasn't responsive to you."

I nodded. An image had come to my mind that I didn't want to tell her. And yet, if I didn't tell, our progess would stall. "I had a picture of something," I said. "It was an image of cutting. Cutting something." That something was flesh, but I didn't want to say so, it was too crazy. And mean. "This whole session seems to have seesawed between hostility and love. I can't help the hostility. It's just there."

"You are discovering ambivalence."

"Am I, Harriet? You think so?" The sarcasm in my voice was unmistakable. I blushed.

After a moment, she said: "You didn't like my interpretation."

"It felt as if you were taking me over, somehow. Labeling me. It felt controlling. Stultifying." I'd said too much, a dull-pencil-eraser sensation overcame me.

"Don't stop," said Harriet.

I shrugged. "Anita could be dominating, but it seems to me now obvious that she just wanted to feel good about herself, which wasn't easy. She had a tough time."

"In lots of ways, she was a mother figure to you."

"Yes."

Harriet looked just like Anita for an instant, swelling large as a Buddha in her chair.

"I've never loved anyone more," I said.

I once house-sat for a man in New Hampshire whose house turned out to be full of guns. Every book on his shelves was about war, as were the videotapes and magazines. In the barn, beside the Ford Taurus, was a genuine World War I jeep. "He trained to go to Korea, but never went," his son explained. "He was too young, and the hostilities were over by the time he was prepared." He's been fixated on fighting ever since.

I didn't train for war. Nor did I really train for achievement. My training, I now saw, was in appreciation. Like Alice Toklas, that's what I did best, I felt. I was good at admiring the other's art—Anita's illustrations, the beautiful light-blue and dark-blue afghan which, before she went to Israel, flowed from her needles in opulent woolen waves. I loved to hold my hands apart while she spooled a hank of fresh wool into a ball. I loved to gaze at the tips of her needles, which made a rubbing, clacking sound and turned like the mouth of an origami fortune-ball, opening with unconscious assurance in this direction and that. More than anything, it was that assurance I craved. "Anita, in Hebrew, means 'He answered,'" Anita once told me. "Ah. Nee-ta." She seemed the answer to me.

I carry her in my mind as the real one, the original, the aleph to my bet, the word to which I am the rhyme, the person whose vision is clear while mine blurs with distortion.

After she moved out of our shared room, I sat in Anita's chair and slept in Anita's bed. Goldilocks broke all the family furniture except what fit her. Yet I wanted Anita to persist. This is the dream that goes unfulfilled: that I can break her and she'll remain, that I can topple her and she'll still be triumphant, that I can rip and punch and bite her and she'll know this is the demon me, the puny me, not the me who loves her, who really loves her—not politely, not for show, but savagely.

I want to tell her, my secret desire, Anita, was that you could be even stronger than you were. I wanted to reveal everything to you. I wanted to bring in the exiled me, the pariah me, from where it was banished under my bed, in the farthest corners of my terrifying closet, in the door that stayed shut even in my dreams because I could not imagine it opening, because even my drowsing self knew I could not keep sleeping if that door opened. I wanted to bring in the part of me that hated you and have you see it and for you still not to withhold from me your smile. Your smile! It lit me like a bulb in a lampshade. If only I could harvest that smile, and dry it, and put it in a box! Oh, a little box like a matchbox, and from time to time when I'm sad and desolate, when the sky is all grainy ash, slide open that little box and take a pinch of you, and have my whole being blossom.

Do we always, to some extent, hate those we love? Hate them because we can never leave them? Hate them because they have so much power over us? Hate them because their heels glow like night-lights and their eyes are boxes of sun? It felt like it was your life or mine, and mine won. You fell and fell, and now you can't keep from falling. If only I were far away! Then I wouldn't see you lean against a walker, having your heavy feet lifted for you.

You once told me that you console yourself with the thought that because you have this disease I probably won't ever get it; the chances seem diminished. This way your life is of some use. I'm in your prayers. When the nurse leaves, and your door is swung open to the hospital corridor, you ask God to keep me safe. Your husband, Mark, our parents, our brothers and their families, me. Could I ever have really hated you? Wasn't it you who taught me to scratch through love's darkness to find the carnival colors pulsing underneath? The blaze in the jack-o'-lantern, the apartments where phosphorescent strangers shone with loneliness, the sense of personal bizarreness, the wild, wild desire to run away from here.

I try to remember ways Anita was mean. Surely she must have been mean, otherwise why would I be so attracted to grumpy women, to demanding landladies and housemates with peroxide hair and an unpleasant manner, to middle-aged students in white big-pocketed blouses who adamantly declare that their problems are unsolvable?

Such women compel me, I now see. I rush to placate them. I bring them valentines, chocolate cakes, compliments on a blue wool coat or scarf, sincere reveries on the talents they display and to which they seem callous. With what vigor they insist on their dissatisfaction! If I could give them their own joy, then we could each have ours, like each person having her own chicken pot pie, her own dinner plate, and nobody grabbing with her fingers the food on someone else's.

The fat women, the clench-faced women, the stubborn women, the scary women—all draw me. I think, Oh, I know how to make her happy, and try what worked with Anita: the Bohack wastebasket, the oddly pleasurable groveling, the reflection back of what, in fact, is spectacular in this woman. When the lion is smiling, she is not eating you. When the lion is letting you pull the splinter from her paw, she is not slashing. Yet I can come up with just one memory of Anita's being nasty to me. It is an almost inconsequential moment.

One childhood summer morning she tripped on the bungalow's concrete steps and went sprawling.

"Are you hurt?" I asked, anxious.

"Of course, you idiot."

Finis.

Although I recall, too, the shamed way I trailed after her like a kicked dog, wondering why I was such a jerk, why, why, I hadn't thought of something intelligent and helpful to say.

"Anita was trouble," a friend of mine remarked.

"How do you know?" I asked, excited.

"It's what you say all the time!"

Anita cracked big sticks across her knee to stoke a campfire. She banked the logs until the fire tipped back its head and roared. She suspected our mother disliked her, that all the other children were her favorite. She suspected our father thwarted her, preferring to satisfy our brothers' ambitions. She was deposed, and deposed again by a torrent of siblings.

I thought of her with her thicket hair, her pilot-light eyes, her enraged impulsiveness, her pointed tactlessness. She was asking for something with her mouth and hands and stomach and stomp-ing, tantrumming feet—but what? The wilder she got, the more my mother shunned her. She saw in her first daughter her own tyrannical mother. What she couldn't confront in her mother, she left unanswered in her daughter. Scalding tears, doors flung shut, hungers that no quantities of food could satisfy, something avid and wanting worked its way through Anita, and her way of reach-ing out was pushing away.

I walked around Levitan's bungalow colony with her when she returned from months of camp—my heroine! Suntanned, reeking of wood smoke and pinesap, the muscles in her legs like bowling balls, her hair a warren. She said, "Oh, how could she do this to me? Look how fat I've got! It was her—I was doing so well! I'd lost so much weight on Weight Watchers, but she said I had to go. And look at me now. All they feed you are starches! There's a loaf of bread at every meal. They pass it around, they keep filling the basket. Yellow margarine as soft as mayonnaise. Spaghetti, vanilla ice cream, sloppy joes on hamburger buns, Kool-Aid in a tin pitcher. It tastes good in that pitcher! And I was thirsty. Empty, empty, stupid calories. She did this to me," she said, punching her leg.

I skipped alongside to keep up, marveling at her words, struck by her beauty. "What are you doing a little jig about?" she said. "What's the matter with you?"

"But Anita—you look, you look great."

She snorted. "If everyone were as blind as you."

"No, Anita. You do. I'm so happy you're home!"

She laughed. "You're her favorite child. That's always been obvious."

"But that's just not true! We both are. That's what she always says."

"Blind, blind, blind," Anita replied, but she grabbed my hand nonetheless, and swung it while she sang a new Girl Scout song: "White snow-white sailing boats on a blue sea.

High in the heavens are clouds floating free.

If I could fly away,

If I might fly away,

Sailing and sailing

What pleasure would be!"

"When I worked for the State," Anita said recently, "I went to the bathroom one day. As I was leaving it, I slipped on a wet floor. I fell down backwards flat on my back. Then I had a dream. I was at a party where all the walls were green. We were laughing and having fun. But then people started to leave. I heard a voice say, 'The party's over.' I woke up. I was lying on my back. Nobody had come to help me. They just continued to do their jobs. Later, X-rays were performed on my hand. It was determined that the very tips of my fingers were gone."

"What do you mean, 'gone'?" I ask.

"They were gone."

"Were you bleeding?"

"No, it happened inside me. In my fingers. The bone was sheared off."

"Ah."

People are leaving. She can't quite reach what she needs.

I try to reconcile the strong Anita to the weak one, the adored Anita to the stultifying one, the Anita who really lives, and the one I seem to be forever inventing. Nothing matches. Always I feel I'm lying. Everything is too absolute, but I don't believe the truth lies somewhere in the middle. The truth rarely lies somewhere in the middle. Is it true I wanted her to fall? As often as I say it, I take it back. As often as I say she wasn't oppressive, I disbelieve. She is a thimble and the Empire State Building, vague as a photo of a photo of a photo, and clear as lightning—a forty-two-year-old woman who told me on Friday she painted a jewelry box in occupational therapy. "I painted one side of it pink, and then on another side I used yellow," she said. Could this be the person who had such a drastic effect on me? I would like to kiss her too hard, a kiss that lets me feel her teeth underneath.

Somehow we are forever sitting side by side and caressing one another in the bodies we once had. This is the scroll-story constantly uncoiling, the truth as it persists, a fantasy that captures the big reality. Anita stretches her arm out to expose the silken blue of her inner elbow, where the vein leaps toward the surface and the body is most sensitive. "Right there," she murmurs. "Ah. Nice. Good, Bonnie."

It is New Year's Eve, and, taking a break from reading, I stand up and try to untangle the briar patch of Anita's hair. I dip my comb in water and work as carefully as I can. The knots are hungry spiders with hard centers. Anita's eyes are tearing. "Shhh," she says, as if I'm being loud, not rough. "Shhh."

"Okay," I say, dipping my comb. There's more knots than hair. I sink the comb's teeth into the edge of a knot and pull, holding the top of her hair with my other hand. "Just think—by next year, your hair will be smooth. Anita, this time don't let the knots grow back."

"Shhh," she says.

"No, listen, Anita. You don't have to go through this again. Don't let the knots come back. They always want to come back, but this time, don't let them."

"I can't help it," says Anita.

"Of course you can. Just remember to brush behind you. Just remember people can see that, too."

"I don't want to think about people seeing me all the time. That's their business. I can't live like that."

"Of course you can. It's so easy. Just—"

"How do you know? You don't know anything, Bon! You live in this world like a blind person. You can't even see what's in front of your own nose."

I see your knots, I think, but remain silent.

"Ouch! That's exactly what I mean!" she says. "Look at what you're doing! Try to see it. Look inside each knot."

Her hair floods reddish brown in the lamplight and swarms with knots. For a moment, it is an impossible task: untangle this by midnight. But then I take a breath. The comb's long teeth plunge slowly.

"That's better," Anita murmurs.

I work as kindly as I can, and Anita knows it's always an accident when my hand slips.

BEAUTY FROM THE UNDERWORLD

At the age of forty-one, I became visible. I was drawn, briefly, to a man who cared how I looked. Up until then being inconspicuous—even liberatingly unkempt—was native to me. I shuffled around the neighborhood in smudged glasses and my husband's big green puffy pants, half submerged in the scenes I'd been writing, blinking at my neighbors through smeared fingerprints. Only on the rarest of occasions did I wear makeup. Mostly the stuff lay stowed in the linen closet, where it turned as cracked and hard as watercolor tiles in its blue-floral tea cozy of a bag—a pouch with a sprung wire that scratched my hands whenever I reached for a pillowcase. Even on Saturday night, when my husband and I went out, I usually wore the trousers his mother gave me for Hanukkah—high-waisted Perma-Prest affairs with an almost comical button floating above my navel and falling in billowing columns over my toes. My hair was a dark, chopped wedge.

The truth was that my husband and I were benignly oblivious of how I looked. What counted was who I was—what I thought and said. We'd met in college. I'd revered feminists and intellectuals—Susan Sontag with her skunk streak and bulky sweaters, Gloria Steinem with her unstained face as honest as raw pine. Concern for one's appearance reflected, I believed, a sort of spiritual malady as debilitating as a limp.

95

But then came this flirtation, this captivation and rearrangement of my internal electrical field, and suddenly I owned a silvery Lycra skirt and leather boots, and I stood hyperventilating in Sephora on Prince Street. For, having become aware that in certain contexts I might actually appear beautiful, that beauty wasn't only for the moronically superficial or congenitally lucky (as I'd heretofore convinced myself), and having discovered, furthermore, what it felt like to be seen, to have craved eyes upon me, I had, at the same time and to my vast dismay, discovered my own abundant physical flaws, the wrinkles etched in my forehead, the age spot set like an asterisk above my right eye. What could I buy that would fix this? What would change me to how I'd been when I felt transformed by beauty?

I wandered up and down the twinkling aisles, unsure of what to buy and wishing that I could seize it all. An assistant fixed me with an assessing glance, made suggestions, switching her hips as she walked ahead of me up the glimmering path. She smiled as I gazed into the glass at the alterations the products worked. Ultimately, I bought four or five items; the prices alone were dazzling. My bounty included a translucent face powder like lustrous skin pollen and a mocha Vincent Longo lipstick that seemed an emblem of sultry, confident femininity. Then home I went.

Could I look, here, as I had in the glittering emporium? Or did the urbane face only live there? As it turned out, it did not. Amazingly, I had brought that face home with me. The stuff worked. In the glass stood the woman whom the man I was involved with seemed to see. The mirror showed a woman with a plush mouth, cheekbones, and blue eyes that knew a secret I didn't.

I tossed out the old stuff—teal shadow, candy-pink rouge, Cyndi Lauper colors I'd bought at a Sears fifteen years earlier. They now seemed like the touch-up hues on a rotogravure. Then I threw out the tea-cozy bag too with its crabbed, stabbing wire like a defective brassiere—for it seemed like the repository of an old concept of myself, one in which I was a plain, dutiful, invisible girl, someone sisterly or maternal, engulfed by a kind of furniture cover of sturdy dull fabric.

For the next three months I was a girl in a pointillist painting—shimmering, thrilled, my skin a skein of electric dots and dashes trying to signal to me something of which, for half my life, I'd been oblivious. I bought an eyelash clamp. I pierced my ears. On the subway I stared at the exquisite plum-glossed lips of an Asian girl. Where had she found that tint? Another woman had fascinating eyebrows, thick, plush. *The brows are the frames of the face*, I repeated to myself, a dictum discovered in a makeup book.

I wanted, I wanted—to be looked at, to be seen. Oh, to be beautiful! I'd always assumed that the superficial was of only superficial importance, not that one's soul glimmered across one's skin. Now, at forty-one, it seemed otherwise. I became one of the appearance obsessed, studying *Hair Style* magazine at the Barnes & Noble. How did Jennifer Aniston do that thing? I must have been the last woman in America to ask.

Everywhere I looked, beauty glimmered as if it had been rained over the city and was vanishing down a thousand grates. Exquisite women slipped out the subway doors, strode off elevators, stepped into the wheeling glass compartments of revolving doors, as if beauty itself were always disappearing—a seduction, a promise, a yearning, a lack. I was left contemplating an odd collection of features I coveted—lips, brows, eyelids, feet. All I wanted to do was shop. I couldn't sit still at my desk long enough to think. And my writing had hardened, clumping into garlands of verbiage. I could no longer vanish down the rabbit holes of words. How foolish my work seemed! Make believe, intellectualization. What mattered was the body.

"You look great," said the man who cared about my appearance. He stared, smiling, and drew the cigarette from his lips.

But unease flared inside me. My guilt at indulging this flirtation grew ever more acute. And I could not really believe that my years of invisibility had been wasted. After all, they'd been full of intellectual adventures that brought truths. I missed being able to think. My marriage, too, was fulfilling in so many ways. I loved my husband, and felt known by him. Yet what should I make of the shocking discovery that you can be drawn to the surface of yourself like fish rushing to the surface when food is sprinkled? I seemed to contain a thousand mouths.

My personality felt kidnapped. I was at war with myself. *Appearance does not matter*, my heels banged forth even as I dashed back to the mirror to see which face peered out. Would it be the familiar round homey old one? Or the long new one with the knowing eyes, the one considered "beautiful"? The mirror figure floating in a matching but backwards bathroom never indicated who would be there next time. After a season I cut off contact with the man who told me he liked my looks. But I was left no longer really even knowing my own hair color. Was it chestnut veined with gray? Or was it the blonde I'd found at the salon? Was I somehow still beautiful, as I'd momentarily been? I recalled the first patient of talk therapy, Anna O., described in *Studies on Hysteria*. She'd looked down at her brown dress and called it blue, her eyes seeing the fabric she'd sewn exactly a year ago. In fact, she often perceived herself to be doing what she'd done exactly a year ago, her brain exposing old images, her eyes seeing herself clad in the past.

I too couldn't sort myself. Sometimes my husband said, with an indulgent smile, "You're wearing makeup!" It made me feel like some dear, pathetic creature who'd made an effort. I lived again in my big green pants. But I wondered constantly about that giddy woman who stood across Lexington Avenue in a short black dress, pulse banging in her wrists and up her arms. I'd never met her before and yet she sprang out of me, and now she was gone and I missed her, although her dress hung in my closet.

Could I get her beauty back? How? The answer was not in the mirror or at Sephora or in the underworld of transgression, which in New York runs as continually as the subways. Beauty lived in the eye of the beholder, and my beholder was gone.

I met my husband senior year of college. On weekends we cooked omelets—which seemed exotic then—throwing in green peppers, onions, Monterey Jack cheese, cracked black pepper, mushrooms, and then clamping a lid on top while the whole thing rose in its cast-iron skillet over a steady flame, quadrupling in size into a frothy delectable wheel so big it seemed some beneficent force must be adding ingredients under the tight lid. We sat at a picnic table in his back yard and ate for hours, talking about everything, getting up to saw off slices of the yeast bread his housemate baked and smearing them with the butter that lived on the kitchen table on a plate. He was a grand storyteller, full of tales of Berkeley, where he'd lived on a semester off, surviving on the popcorn at the movie theater where he changed the marquee, singing in Spanish at the Cheesecake Factory where all the other workers were Mexican, making his own way. When he told stories, leaning toward me across the table, describing subtleties of texture and tone, I felt lucky. What gifts of perception and expression he possessed! It felt like the gateway to a marvelous intimacy.

After we married, I wondered if Augustine was right and it was blasphemy to love my husband so much. A Georgia O'Keeffe painting borrowed from the library hung on the wall opposite our bed. It had big white iron petals with the yellow of the pollen caked thick as halvah on the stamens. Checking out art from the library had been my husband's idea. I liked knowing that each canvas had a brown envelope glued invisibly to its back. It seemed like a secret connection to a private world, a little pouch of self tucked from view, happy evidence that we'd made use of the resources at hand. And it was typical of my husband to discover and provide the incentive for this fun thing—art borrowing! The view from our bed changed every two months, and I even liked toting the framed print back to the library because then we could chose something else—purple and blue Chagalls with floating brides, Paul Klee fish, Miró moons and hooks and eyelike emblems—a catalogue of dreams, a secret language we loved but defied translation and which beckoned like our own future.

In Brooklyn, years later, my husband was still extravagantly wonderful company, but something seemed lacking. I could be anyone tagging along beside him. I felt like a sidekick, a pal, a good, affectionate dog standing on my hind legs to lick his face. At a friend's wedding my husband and I found ourselves sitting on the lush green lawn with a woman whose own husband had stayed home. While my husband spoke, this woman smiled. Her head bobbed eagerly as if on a spring, and her expression of delight seemed both sincere and yet set in place. My husband grew expansive; he brimmed with joy. I thought: *I'm like her. She could replace me and I could just step away. What my husband needs is a smiling, receptive woman—it never needed to be me.* This thought was both devastating and liberating.

Not long after this I met the man who liked how I looked. Now that he was gone I no longer could return to my old inconspicuousness, for it no longer felt like invisibility but ugliness.

"I need you to let me know. Do you like how I look?" I asked my husband.

"Yup," he said. "You look good all the time."

"Well, if you think it, tell me." Still, he almost never did. He'd come from a family where compliments were rare and sarcasm frequent.

Without the mirror of that other man's eyes, my own sense of self started to depart like the pupil of a person going walleyed. One part of me felt twisted away, while another stared straight ahead. Things had too many dimensions or too few. I craved to once again be that beautiful girl I'd been but didn't want to leave my marriage. It seemed my beauty lived on the staircase to that man's apartment—the higher I ascended it the more beautiful I became until his eyes saw me and the transformation was complete. But this was filching beauty, shoplifting love, behaving like someone feral, desperate, undeserving, nasty within. I couldn't do it anymore. Nor could I pick up my home life where I'd left off.

I saw now that I'd been asleep under my pot lid, cozy, shut away in my cubicle, beguiling myself with complicated thoughts, not suspecting I was becoming like the professor in *Strange Interlude*—"a refugee from reality." The snug, safe life had suited me. The fire of the stove was warm and it had been nice to have armor all around. But that life no longer worked. The world kept calling my name—in the way a woman and a man kissed on the 5 train, in the smile a husband gave his wife in front of a brownstone down the street. Longing stretched within me, then snapped with a horrible pang.

I went to a meeting of Co-Dependents Anonymous, a twelve-step group that met in a hospital. I wasn't quite sure why I'd come. An acquaintance with sympathetic eyes had gone away for a month to Italy. I'd been a visiting writer at a university class he taught, and we'd gone out to dinner together after. He wasn't the man with whom I'd been involved, nor had our friendship been more intense than a spate of e-mails about humanist psychology, a topic of mutual interest. "I'm going to enjoy looking at the beautiful women of Milan," he wrote on the eve of his departure. "Surely as a single man I can acknowledge that." His remarks stung unreasonably, and I realized that I would likely have no more to do with him upon his return.

Still, when he left I felt devastated, as if life now had no meaning. Obviously this was an overreaction to his departure, I informed myself while I wept. It was August in New York; only a few solitary figures moved down the blistering streets. A hot white sun pulsed in a gluey sky. Life was elsewhere. I thought of the dental phenomenon of "referred pain," where one tooth is decayed but a different tooth hurts. I recalled the endodontist coming at me with a big gray ice cube held with tongs. "It's the only way we can really determine where the problem is," he said as he pushed the ice cube into my mouth. "Here?" he said, sliding the ice. "Here?" I rocketed out of the seat, pain blazing to the root of my heels, then throbbing with a long half-life.

"See? It wasn't the tooth you came in pointing to," he explained kindly to my leaky eyes.

This Italy-bound man had inadvertently touched some integral, intense hurt. But I didn't like the idea of a man I barely knew going away and making me feel he'd pulled all the meaning of life after him like a person turning in bed, obliviously taking the blankets. So I started attending these meetings, which concerned getting free from emotional bondage. The group declined to give a definition for the term "co-dependent"—perhaps to avoid providing an excuse to exclude those who would gain by attending meetings—but I identified with many of the traits on the handout sheet under the heading "compliance patterns": "I minimize, alter, or deny how I truly feel." "I give up my truth to gain the approval of others or to avoid change." "I have to be needed in order to have a relationship with others." (Something that had been far truer when I was younger.) Many of the people in the meeting were involved with drug addicts or alcoholics. I couldn't say quite why I was here and yet the statements people made caused eerie resonances within me.

Beneath the hospital's fluorescent lights our skin glinted, and we all seemed to be wearing dingy jeans and thrift-shop sneakers—a gathering of the marginal, the peripheral, the figures who lurk in the corner of one's eye. In the beginning I told myself, "This isn't really me" as I've often told myself at beginnings. To my surprise, a full half of those gathered here were men. We went around the circle and each person spoke for four minutes. It was all anonymous except for your first name. People from all walks of life—some hardscrabble people with a cardboard belt and grubby vinyl jacket, but a few quite obviously well-to-do, with Versace bags and face-lifts—each talking briefly, but with utmost honesty. Many "shares" had the quality of the last four minutes of a therapy session, when there was no time to lose and one must arrive at the heart of the matter. You weren't allowed to say anything afterwards: "no crosstalk," and no advice. It was what it was, and then the next person spoke.

Stories of remote or impervious partners, of perfectionist parents and parents who'd vanished into addictions, of choosing as lovers people interred in sadness or anger or booze or marriage to someone else, of compulsively trying to control one's environment (I thought of my pot lid) or other people (I thought of the truths I'd never shared with my husband both for fear of his reaction and because if I said them they'd seem real). There were other stories, too, ones that taught me about joy—stories of tango dancing, of reading to a daughter *The Little Engine That Could*, of spontaneous poetry and hard-earned restraint. Aria after aria, each four minutes long, and I sang my aria too. And in this cruelly lit place full of maskless, ghostly figures who somehow seemed like vestigial selves, as if I'd come to some kind of storeroom of souls, I began to recover my sense of beauty.

"Hi, Bonnie," said a few of the people in the group when I came to my third meeting. I blinked. They remembered my name! The people here connected me to what I'd said before—the truths I'd blurted, the longings to which I'd given voice; these starkly lit people were accumulating me, the truest parts of me, and didn't forget me from week to week. As I didn't forget them—the man who always had a ringing in his ears, the woman who came in pushing a shopping cart full of yellowing papers, the social worker with the impish, knowing, sexy smile, yes, him most of all. His eyes had a gleaming, triangular, goatish quality, and his hair was salt-and-pepper, professionally trim, and he often ran the meetings, turning the laminated pages, knowing how to be judicious and genial, both, in keeping the meeting on task. It seemed to me that he said my name with a special regard, before shifting his attention to the next person in the circle, and I discovered once again the depth of my craving and how unworthy of a certain kind of male attention I felt—fatherly attention, it must be—and how glorious when I received it. I recalled that when I was a nursery-school child I'd told myself I didn't need my father's attention. He sat in his dark gray cashmere greatcoat in our playroom, the aroma of winter clinging to him, watching my brothers wheel about on their bicycles, and my older sister dressed as a princess in blue tulle and a glittering tiara. "I'm free because I don't need him," I'd told myself—and I'd felt free, but cold. I expected to warm up soon. It occurred to me I hadn't warmed up yet, although I was already in my forties. How misguided I'd been to believe I didn't need his attention because I could survive without it. The craving for his attention had pained me as a child, and so I recanted it. But now it was back upon me. I talked about this when my turn came. At the end, as if we were still children, we formed a circle and held hands. I was holding hands with a woman missing a joint of her thumb and a man who was an acerbic lawyer. His mother, when he was a boy, controlled him with the threat she'd send him to a lunatic asylum. We chanted the serenity prayer and then some other jingles. I always felt exultant by the end.

After the meeting I walked west on light rubber heels, past two hushed green parks and a chapel where a gospel chorus sang to empty pews, the windows thrown open. Often I stopped to listen to the chiming voices, feeling radiant with gratitude. The city no longer felt populated by strangers because I was hearing so many of other people's secrets. Everyone was a hidden envelope, a tucked-away pouch. On the subway I was calmer, and if my eyes met a weary woman across the aisle, or a father soothing his child, we exchanged a smile. People no longer seemed so alien and scary and insubstantial, and neither did I.

And then I started wearing the clothing I'd bought during my carnival time. A short suede skirt. A tight green top. The faux-alligator boots. My husband smiled, a private appraising smile. "All dressed up," he might say. "Mm-hmmm," I'd answer. But if he didn't respond for some reason or another, it no longer defeated me. Somehow—from going to the meetings, perhaps—I was no longer dependent on him to feel beautiful. Wearing my new clothing—the ankle boots of mauve suede with contrasting leather tips, the black ones with the inner zipper—gave me a novel confidence.

"You look like you take yourself more seriously, like you are holding yourself to a higher standard," remarked my husband one evening when I came home from teaching. I realized that I did take myself more seriously, as if it mattered how others saw me and how I saw myself. I no longer felt like a shambling, unworthy child who didn't warrant attention—for this had been the secret message of my father's obliviousness that my heart had well understood. Being seen—by the man who'd found me beautiful, by the anonymous attendees of the hospital meeting—had cured something ashamed in me. The entire world, strangely, seemed more visible, as if it too had been drawn more closely to the surface. I noticed fabrics and textures, the extravagant beauty of our city.

I often wore a silver bracelet I bought in Arizona. This bracelet felt like a totem, something lucky and magical. When my husband did make me feel beautiful, then it was as if we shared a secret between us, a private energy field with the current shimmering back and forth. When he didn't, I could remind myself of the secret, which still existed. I glanced at the bracelet and remembered where I'd first seen it, on a blanket spread on the red earth in Arizona, presided over by a Native American woman with silver baubles that could be trinkets or treasures. Their value was what you saw in them. I'd bought this bracelet for ten dollars, but when my glance fell on it, a blessing flashed up, a wink.

I no longer felt invisible. A mirror had somehow gotten propped up inside. I existed, occasionally smart, certainly flawed, but more and more real. I could see now that my husband was basically shy about compliments; it didn't mean he didn't see me. Having yearned to be seen by his own parents, who'd ignored him almost on principle, he wasn't at ease giving praise. I learned to notice the more subtle signals—his glinting, sunny gaze, the nod of approval when I stood up for myself, the way he brought me a sack of apricot-centered butter cookies he'd bought because he knew I adored them, the way he gave me the window seat on railroad trips so I had the better view. Now I could see what had been invisible—his specific attraction for my specific self. It really had been there all along.

I had chosen a man who didn't give compliments but for a long time I didn't notice because I didn't believe I deserved them. But then they arrived, brought to me by someone else, and altered me in a molecular way. It was a sea change—an elemental reconstitution. There was no way to return to the old pattern.

These days it seems to me that the body is a purse clasping the soul of the self, and the soul is always changing. Its nature is metamorphosis. It can't stay in its cubicle cocoon forever without withering. We betray ourselves if we don't set forth. Now, teaching a class, riding the subway, my glance falls on my bracelet, and a reassuring gleam winks up from it—a last echo of the man who cared how I looked, and a reminder of my husband's actual desire for my particular company, and of the girl whose desire for beauty was long locked away, a secret even from herself.

Becoming Visible

I wrote the essay about beauty, and my involvement with that man, but it wasn't enough. Something had been left out. And it couldn't be wedged into the earlier essay. I had to write a second, with a different tone, in order to name it.

A man kissed me on a subway platform, and, just as in a fairy tale, nothing was the same again. It was a Tuesday night in mid-October. A moist chill clung to the air. My husband and I had been living back in New York for two years. The man was a distant colleague, a stranger really. At an after-work gathering, he'd invited me to try a green drink—chartreuse. The liquor carried a scent of spring grass, tasted of basil and kerosene, and had a kind of psychotropic wormwood intoxication. The three-color process that constitutes reality slid out of synch; rims of red and yellow celluloid hemmed everything. Then he'd walked me to the subway station and we'd stood on the platform, chatting.

"Don't you want to be on the other side?" he eventually inquired, pointing. I squinted. An extra set of tracks lay beyond the ones near my feet, like an extra horizon line. I spun around: a brick wall loomed where a set of rails should have been. But I'd grown up in the Bronx, knew uptown from down before I knew the seasons! And then, in what seemed a shocking act, the man closed the space between us in a kiss, and our mouths opened.

I had to sit. It surprised me how solidly planted the steel tracks were in their ditches. So straight. Everything else was in motion, swinging again and again into place. "We have the same hair," he said, smiling. But I silently noted mine was tinged with gray. "How old are you?" he inquired, but I didn't want to say. He was eight years younger than I was. A train came thundering into the station and I jumped aboard, leaving behind a gold-rimmed opera stub on which I'd scrawled my phone number but with one digit possibly wrong. I couldn't remember if my number was 49 or 79. "May I call you?" asked the man as the doors hung open. "Better not," I answered. "Maybe I'll call you. Let me see how I feel when the chartreuse wears off." I phoned him three days later, although the chartreuse had not faded. Months later a trace still ran in my veins.

"Cotton underpants are boring," he said a month after we met. We were lying on his bed. "So is this white bra. Silk is sexy. Why don't you ever wear a dress? Or makeup?"

What a piggish, obnoxious boor! I exclaimed to myself, at the same time surprised that he registered my underthings. Wasn't the whole point of them simply to come off? It seemed bizarre of him. I'd traveled here just for sex and had told him so. Sex with a stranger, it seemed to me, would obliterate a certain corrosive longing that plagued me. In my twenties I'd had boyfriends, and sex had been something good and salutary. In recent years the body itself had gathered a strange hunger, an incessant, continual dark, distracting longing.

"What I want is perfectly normal," he said. "Did you know that half of all Victoria's Secret catalogues go to men?"

I did not.

"It doesn't cost a million to look like a million," he said, mortifyingly plucking the underpants from the crack in my behind.

I sat up, reaching for my shirt. "I dress the way I do because I respect myself," I said.

And later, standing in an ATM cubicle beneath a fluorescent glare that I was sure converted my face to sandpaper, I vowed "I'll never see him again." Relief rushed in with the icy air as the door swept open behind me.

But then, on an impulse, and because I did not want to return to my accustomed sequestered life in which I now realized I felt like a sock lost under the bed, that Friday I pulled on a black sheath dress. I purchased an orange packet of No Nonsense off-black pantyhose, stepped into high heels, and even extracted from the back of the linen closet a fifteen-year-old blue floral cloth pouch of cosmetics bought during grad school. Rose lipstick. Black sunglasses.

He grinned across Lexington Avenue. "You look great!" And smoked his cigarette, staring, as I crossed the street.

I flushed. It had never really occurred to me as a possibility—that I could pull off being a girl. Girls, by the way, were what he called the gleaming females he was attracted to, slightly swell-cheeked, young, sporting spaghetti-strapped tops and streaked hair, or clad in office attire—a starched blouse with tiny earrings glinting like the tips of teeth—the word itself implying an obliviously self-possessed, iron-strong sprite. Girl. Whereas a woman was this other thing, out of his mouth: stolid, ladyish, dull as the pillar lodged under the pediment of a bank. Sexist? Yes, I thought so. But it did not diminish his force.

And so it began. A blue brassiere the shade of morning glories. A black slip. Cocoa-colored lipstick that drifted off my lips like mayonnaise. The quizzical clamps of the eyelash curler, in appearance half-speculum, half-orthodontic vise, and conjuring in one's hand an iron sun half sunk in an invisible sea. Standing in line at Club Monaco holding a $198 black V-neck cashmere sweater—demented by the price of everything—I could scarcely catch my breath. Only one girl stood ahead of me but the cashier did everything in extreme slow motion—unclasping the white plastic bar locked on a garment, drawing the charge card through her machine.

I hadn't eaten all day (food was superfluous, counterproductive) and my heart had begun to bang in my chest; the store's walls themselves seeming faintly to suck in and out with each breath as I clutched my prize—this expensive stitch of goat's wool which, in the fitting room, found a delicacy to my throat that transformed me into someone so aristocratically pretty I had to have it at once. Sooner than at once. I needed to be out on the street with it in my bag a minute ago. It felt as if—it really felt as if—I would be beautiful insofar as I owned this thing. It seemed in fact the one exquisite object on this planet, and if I didn't own it immediately there was no chance for me.

The same thing in Macy's. In Bloomingdale's. In Victoria's Secret with its palisades of rose and tiger-stripe and ivory brassieres, its merry widows and voluptuous balcony bras, its chorus-line racks of nighties reminiscent of French chambermaids and schoolgirls—I couldn't grab things fast enough. The whole time I was internally gasping. How many times did I stand beside two or three other girls chomping gum, sighing, waiting for the clerk with her pink curlicue key ring to unlock a changing room, and all the while desperately hoping that at least one or two of the items in my fists would do that thing, that thing which made me sigh, "Oh. Yes," because the figure in the glass looked like someone snipped from a magazine. And the disappointment when one bra after another was dowdy, didn't work. The rumpled or massive cups, the saggy chest, the breasts brimming the top like over-risen dough—a hundred ways in which the body can look ungainly, and all seeming to present a verdict that the truth is this familiar ugliness, and that a lovely-making object is rare almost to the verge of being nonexistent and so, no matter the cost, worth every penny.

Madame Bovary and the merchant Lheureux. The gnome who sets the dungeon tasks yet knows the way to freedom. The frog who requires only a kiss—or is it marriage?—to retrieve the princess's golden ball which was swallowed by the mire. The shops seemed to grant the secret wish I didn't know I was wishing. They offered magic beauty. They drew me and then clasped me ever closer. I did not recognize myself.

For a desperation had kindled in me like the suck of a pilot light grabbing a flame. I would get it into my head that I must have a lip-liner pencil in "raisin." Or translucent face powder. Or a really true-red lipstick (I now subscribed to *Allure*, and scoured *Glamour* and *Vogue* and even *Seventeen* for tips). I haunted Sephora, marveling at the women rolling their lips together before a mirror, stroking shadow into the eyelid crease. It seemed mysterious almost to the point of requiring a kind of miracle, to find the right color that would suit me. Which of the black-smocked, red-lipped models from an old Robert Palmer video would know the answer?

And why this pulsing impatience day after day? Was it that I didn't allow enough time for these expeditions? Or was it that the shine and glitter of the emporia themselves aroused to the point of distraction—the way bookstores with their glossy jackets once did, each object reflective as a glazed cake from Payard, the surfaces imperturbably sealed and seeming to contain within a composed, complete, and almost impossible beauty—so that I could barely tolerate to stand amidst the tantalizing glimmer of Sephora, surveying the tiered battalion of lipsticks with their celestially smooth, steeply beveled facets, the pots of foundation cream arrayed in the subtlest spectrum of skin, the oversized backlit bottles lining the walls and named for powers and cravings: Envy. Beautiful. Poison.

Obsession. Each one presided, squat, in an elevated niche. Standing before them, I had the mad thought that if I could just drink each elixir, glug that nectar, then I would possess its mystic trait inside me forever.

Because the more I became a girl the more anxious about my girlhood I became. It was always vanishing. I pierced my ears, whitened my teeth, waxed my brows, cauterized my skin tags, varnished my toenails, bought silvery bracelets for my wrists, highlighted my hair, learned to use Blonde Ambition and Frizz Ease and Wind Down Relaxing Creme and a flat iron and a gust of spray (spritz the air, walk through the cloud) for my hair, which by now lapped my shoulders. The very color of my hair had become a mystery to me. I couldn't tell if I looked like a blonde or a blonde wannabe, a pretty woman or a cracked hag. Was I the young girl or the crone she swivels into? Of course, merchants get rich offering women aspects of their own alienated selves, and on some level I knew this. But X adored me in my new garments, and so, then, did I. Rapture of angora, of silk, of fur, of hair. A ball of sun flung itself when the revolving door spun, racing away over the display cases and upturned mirrors—and I hastened after it.

I'd been incarnated into time. Before the chartreuse I thought of myself as appearing a cute thirty-two. Now I saw the gray saturating my hair and the lines corrugating my brow. When, at the beginning of our acquaintanceship, on our very first afternoon, X had turned up overdressed in a houndstooth jacket and argyle sweater and beard and small neat black Reeboks, he'd reminded me of my irritating and otiose brother-in-law. The very idea of making an effort to please him by wearing special clothing, as he suggested, had merely brought a sardonic smirk to my lips. How demeaning for an adult, an intellectual, to indulge in a game of dress-up. Now, I refused to see him sans cosmetics, and often during the course of a visit I would withdraw to the bathroom and unzip my case. The makeup itself seemed an aspect of sex.

"You own me," I told him. "It works both ways," he said. Still, I wanted him not to see the stony truth of me, which was that at home I was often lumpish, mucus-throated, clad in big green sweatpants and a ratty sweater and wearing tortoiseshell eyeglasses that made my skin itself look darkly furred, as if I'd sprouted a layer of hair, as if I were half simian. "You're a beast in a frilly dress!" an ex-boyfriend once said to me affectionately, and I tended to agree.

And now, becoming a girl, I felt all the prototypical shyness of a girl—I didn't understand frankly where exactly the allure came from or how X so reliably transitioned from the domesticity of eating mac-and-cheese to stroking me, lying in a bedroom illuminated with candles in glasses the size of milk bottles that created a flickering space reminiscent of a mission shrine.

I was aware of the feminist statement that to be a woman is to be a female impersonator, and in fact I'd been amazed when Naomi Wolf's *The Beauty Myth* reached bestseller status back in 1991—surely nobody still needed to be informed that our models of beauty are toxic. Hadn't we all heard about the arsenic mixed into the kohl? I'd read Beauvoir's opus when I was at the Bronx High School of Science, riding the jouncing 12 bus home from class.

Vast as a loaf of honey cake, bound in a simple shiny white cover stamped with the colossal words *The Second Sex*, it was a text possible to absorb only slowly, the narrow-set lines on aerogram paper themselves titrating into one a sensation of intelligence, of lucidity, of almost otherworldly transport, until it seemed that to be the Other meant to be the particular Parisian priestess whom one admired while reading her book, jolting along on the bus. A certain perfumed opacity constituted an aspect of the sibyl's professed imprisonment. For Beauvoir enacted a paradox. She argued against the feminine mystique but seemed in her prose, with its ineffable sinuous nuance, its commanding insistence on style, to embody that very mystique—as if in fact beauty truly *is* essential to being a woman, even as one attractively denies it.

And there was a second paradox, too, in which she was implicated, and it now involved me. She pointed out how, when a Colette heroine falls in love: "A conflict breaks out between her original claim to be a subject, active, free, and, on the other hand, her erotic urges and the social pressure to accept herself as a passive object... Oscillating between desire and disgust, between hope and fear, declining what she calls for, she lingers in suspense between the time of childish independence and that of womanly submission."

Submission! Could that still be true? Must one submit in order to be a woman? Even this late in our history? As a high school girl bouncing along on the 12 bus home from Bronx Science, I scoffed. Yet now in my adulthood I discovered it *was* still true. There was a delirium to the inner collapse, a shocking pleasure in subjugation.

"What's making you attractive is castrating yourself," opined a male friend. He was a devotee of psychoanalysis, a concert pianist who favored a black turtleneck and a warlock's medallion. "It's basic Freud. Female masochism is normal adult female sexuality. To accept your boyfriend's phallus you must emasculate yourself, hence your present anxieties. Read Helene Deutsch."

I declined to do so, as if she might be the ice queen who would glaze all the living figures of my inner carnival, the jealous stepmother whose cold eyes would paralyze. Now I consciously chose the ecstasy of being dominated, if that's what it was. For I'd found that the more you are attracted to a man, the less he resembles your otiose ex-brother-in-law. And the more he can give you something you can reach no other way, something that isn't even sexual, isn't even womanly.

For some neglected, feral little girl in me sprang up in his arms. I'd thought I'd done with this awful girl forever back in high school. I'd transubstantiated her through study, I'd supposed. All those months and years and then decades of composed and then reworked sentences, all those papers and stories and essays and even books, weren't they really pavilions in which I could change out of that girl? That girl with her greenish skin and palms of dragon scales, the white mackintosh coat her mother dressed her in and the red vinyl beret perched in such a dorky way on her head— wasn't ridding myself of her the whole point of my adulthood? I'd said sayonara to her in high school, under the blazing Lightolier desk lamp. I'd written her out in the pages and pages of legal pad notes before exams. She was stupid, impulsive, lunatic, an absolute embarrassment—and gone, gone, gone, for over two decades. But now she reappeared.

When X smiled at me across Lex as I stood in my little black dress, she blushed and glanced down at the pavement. When we kissed on a bench by the river, she was reaching out through me, grabbing out through me. When he smiled into my eyes, hers moistened and glittered, shoving his love into her, hoarding it. The alchemy of sex brought forth this exile.

And when he stared at me in my pantyhose, the opaque top of the hose embarrassingly like runner's shorts, the waistband biting into the flesh, I felt momentarily more keenly loved than I ever had, which is what I suppose evoked that girl. It had something to do with humiliation and acceptance. For one moment I felt wanted past anything I could connive or engineer, wanted not for contriving a clever mouth or displaying an agile mind, wanted not for any act of personality but for me, my core self, my body, wanted past any performance, any act of will, any effort and therefore fraudulence—wanted perhaps the way a parent might want a child even before the girl's first word, wanted in her elemental self, a self past even her own knowing.

Later, sitting on his blue futon couch that perpetually leaned sideways, gazing toward the silent TV with its defective rim where a ribbon of red and blue smeared the top of the screen, the air around us flickering with the shadows of the starlings that engulfed the tree in his yard, their hundred wings flashing in the window, I longed to remain in my shimmering fantasy world of X and me. I hadn't actually thought I needed love. It had always seemed dweeby and sentimental in songs—"Somewhere out there!"—and I assumed that those who mewled for love had a weak spot like a bruised fruit. Now I found a cramping spasm of need for it inside myself. I wanted to fit into the socket of X's underarm as if that were my true home.

And yet I knew better than to think I could live with him. I actually loved and admired my husband. He had a substantiality that X did not. On X's bulletin board, which hung beside the front door, was tacked an envelope to a Holocaust survivor—someone elderly by now, to be sure—that had been sent to X in error. It had to do with reconstruction payments. The entire time I knew X he never sent the envelope back, although I occasionally asked him about this. My husband would have made it his business to send the envelope back right away, and then would have phoned the German government office to make sure it had been received. Other people were real to my husband—he was a man of the world—in a way they weren't to X.

Yet even what was unviable about X added to his fairy tale allure, isolating him from other women and making him someone about whom I could feel more secure. He lived in an apartment the size of a freight elevator. When I didn't visit, he slept until dark, having gone to bed at six or seven in the morning because he had no job, often leaving his apartment only to go to his therapy sessions, for which his father paid. He would sigh with exasperation—a brown nicotine fog escaping his mouth—at the small demands of life, having to wait for a bus, having to choose between three types of copier paper, all of which had their separate flaws and virtues. Sitting there, I wanted the afternoons to extend into an ever deepening indigo without ever arriving at night; I wanted them simply to titrate in more and more of that hallucinogenic cobalt blue. I breathed shallowly, telling myself, this is not real. No, actually, this is the most real thing of all. No, this is not at all real.

And then my husband found out. I came home after midnight one night.

He was sitting at the kitchen table. "Where were you?" he said.

"At the Barnes and Noble. Like I told you."

"Which one?"

"Eighty-Sixth Street," I said instantly, although my heart had started to pound.

"What did you do after?"

I felt queasy. "Nothing. I came straight home."

"And you're sure it was the Barnes and Noble on Eighty-Sixth Street, right?"

I gazed at him, confused, the blood roaring in my ears. "Of course." What should I say, how could I backtrack? How could I return in time to when I was just walking up the stairs to our door so I could choose a different Barnes and Noble to have been in?

"Baby, that bookstore closed at nine." He stared at me with enormous sad eyes, having waited up alone in the empty house by himself, and my heart broke for him, and terror flooded me as he said: "You are having an affair, and now I know it."

That evening a terrible season began. We talked, wept, hid, felt guilty, felt ill, found one another again. Why had I not been able to feel he was attracted to me? What, from even before the affair, had arisen and was standing between us? Our untruthfulness had not begun the night I met X. There had been secrets before, sentiments I had withheld, sentiments he had, too. And now we discovered what it was to be honest, and thus to become more real to one another and even to ourselves, to become less pulpy and evasive and dissociated and make-believe. We each blurted experiences that seemed ugly and shameful and cruel—feelings we'd wished to spare one another, and ourselves—but which were in fact beautiful simply because true. Strange to discover, but our love really did grow from this. And our marriage did not blow away, as I feared it would from an onslaught of truth.

As for the affair, some part of me was relieved to have it discovered. I hadn't been able to stop it on my own. It had the quality of a delirious addiction I could not quit. I'd been desperately running myself ragged back and forth across the city, with one aspect of myself stowed in Manhattan and the rest in Brooklyn. Riding the subway home I'd shut my eyes, my heart throbbing painfully in fear of discovery and then in childish resentment that I had to live my life like a thief. I didn't know how to give up that dream-come-true fantasy space over the rainbow, the tutti-frutti blur at the top of X's TV screen, even as it was no place I could ever call home. As soon as my husband discovered about it, I was released.

"You've come into your own," say friends. "You carry yourself differently."

"My hair is a different color," I reply.

"No. It's something else. Before you were . . . innocent. There was just a certain naiveté. A giggly quality. A lack of confidence. You're more forceful now."

I nod. It's true I feel less apologetic. Less congenitally embarrassed. I've tossed the grimy, puffy turquoise coat that I assumed people disregarded because appearance was unimportant. I wear lace shirts on occasion. I trust that my instinctive responses are significant. They no longer mortify me. My voice seems louder, even to me. I no longer receive unsolicited advice although, in my previous life, I did constantly. And—can it be unrelated?—I'm more observant of the physical world, the webbed texture of a particular tree trunk, the rasp of my cat's tongue on my throat, his rattling thrum.

I've given up the midnight cab rides and the continual surrendering of my charge card, which during that time flashed like a detachable third shimmering hand. After all those visits to that apartment, the thing that was forever slipping away—an essential beauty—seems to be lodged in me at last, like the big strong knot my sister taught me to tie to root my sewing. You wrap the thread around and around your finger, then slide it off, purposely letting the strands tangle into a thick messy knot. Once grounded, the needle flies up but the thread pulls taut; the stitches add up. That messy time with my husband—of truths admitted, flung out, choked forth, stooped for and retrieved, has also rooted me.

The old sense of inherent shame is gone. I would never have believed that could change. I dress different, I walk different, I feel different: a later bloomer. It was as if I'd stood on tiptoe my whole life, straining for something, living in my upper register, and now my heels rest on the earth. I had been wanted for something past any act of will I might muster, and I felt loved, and lovable to my bones.

I hadn't understood before that sex could do this, nor that honesty could do this either. Now, however, my entire self was in the bedroom when I was—and this included that self hidden even from me: the impetuous, spontaneous, feral one, the one studded with briars and smeared with dried tears, rocking against a schoolyard fence, alone under a churning metal sky. It was as if the beloved had gone back to fetch her, and had cured her loneliness. He let me come home again.

To be accepted and even found beautiful when you forfeit control, when you admit the truth! That alters a person. As does being considered beautiful when you've exerted effort. One's ugliness had been an illusion. It was unnecessary to live with the old beliefs. These days I rarely think about the time when I stood in a pencil silk-lined skirt and brown lipstick, with my hair just done, waiting for a stranger. The air itself was an intoxicant. All of New York wheeled around us, the cabs, the lime-green leaves on the trees, the geyser of yellow forsythia in the florist window, the dingy white cat lolling on the stack of *New York Posts*, the sparrows and grackles fluttering aloft, the sudden snow—no, it was blossoms!—tumbling out of the blue sky. He smiled, flicking his cigarette as he strolled, his eyes finding mine, and all of me looked back, aspects of me rushing to the surface, never entirely to sink away.

And, when I left that time with X behind, I brought what I'd gained with me, an awareness, a solidity, a conviction that one's hungers and wants matter, an expansion of my sense of who I am, and who others are, as well.

THE WATCHER

"Best Ox-Tail Soup," I said to my husband, who was driving the car.

He nodded.

"Best Healthy For You Fish Fry."

His mouth quirked up in a smile, an effort I appreciated. We were both zonked from not getting enough sleep. Jamaican bakeries swung past, their windows advertising fluorescent-yellow-crusted beef pies as well as jerk chicken and sorrel. This was deep in the borough of Queens, where we now coasted along decaying boulevards under a thickening crisscross of power lines. A car with purple-blue windows slid up, dark as a nightclub, throbbing to a slow beat. I bounced a leg to its rhythm and squinted ahead to see the next sign.

"Hillside," I declared with satisfaction. "After that should be Jamaica."

My husband nodded again. We'd been up late trying to decide whether I should apply for a particular job that would mean moving from the Northeast to another part of the country entirely. Paul was all for it, I was less sure. I'd be relinquishing the writing time I now had—but maybe being able to support myself would cure a disequilibrium between Paul and me, I secretly thought. Paul had his own reasons for wanting me to pursue this job. A haze of depression overcame me as I wondered what to do. So it was a comfort, now that we were both weary and in unknown terrain, that all the streets my father had specified appeared right on cue, each in its proper order: Hollis, Murdoch, Linden. I was impressed, as usual, with my father's thoroughness. How much I still had to learn from him, even at this late date. Oh, I did not want to move!

"Your father gives too many directions," Paul suddenly exclaimed. "You can't get the overview!"

I turned, surprised. "Really? That's not at all how I see it." My finger tapped the notebook that held the directions. "The detail my father gives is terrific. You can tell right away if you're lost."

Paul shook his head—clearly perceiving something deeply wrong in my answer—but chose not to respond.

Three weeks earlier, my mother had phoned. "It's customary to go to the graveyard between Rosh Hashanah and Yom Kippur."

"I know, Ma. Count me in," I said, recalling how last year's High Holy Day Sunday at the cemetery had been bustling—so crowded it was almost festive. Some families lunched on deli sandwiches while others had just marble cake and wine, leaning on the cars. An occasional word in Yiddish leapt into the air. Women in shiny dresses and reticent men smoking cigars sauntered dreamily between the headstones and the gritty sunlight twinkled all around. "I'm putting it on my calendar."

But as the date approached my father grew uneasy. "We'll let it go this year," he declared at last. He just wasn't up to it, explained my mother in private. His mood was low. "I understand," I said, because I'd witnessed how the concerns of old age transfixed him. Aside from the myriad physical ailments, there were other problems, emotional ones, or rather metaphysical ones, that he didn't articulate. I offered no advice. How could I know what it was like to be at that particular vantage point gazing off toward whatever promised land came next? Also, in the late autumn of the year before, my sister Anita had passed away. She'd been sick so long, and her departure from life had been so gradual, that even after she'd died I had the sense that she was present in the Bronx, in some room I could still visit.

I offered to take my mother alone, but she said, "No, I'd rather not." And that particular traditional High Holiday Sunday came and went.

But three weeks later the phone rang late on Thursday evening. "It's important to pay one's respects," announced my mother's voice—to my surprise because she doesn't believe in an afterlife.

My father seized the phone and recited the names of all the obscure streets deep in the thicket of Queens that we'd pass, spelling out even the names that weren't tricky: Hillside, Linden. He spoke with a sort of royal asperity, as if he were shifting a sourball in his mouth, and as if something had been resolved within him. Diligent daughter that I was, I took notes.

And then there it rose across Springfield Boulevard, the Old Montefiore Cemetery shimmering with the last bronze leaves of autumn. We swung across four empty lanes and up toward the brick guardhouses, and there stood my mother in a pink top and black trousers, peering into the distance. Paul honked but she stared obliviously past us into the gray October day like a sailor squinting for the shoreline—a short woman with a high sweep of beauty-parlor-burnished hair. She took steno for a law office in the Bronx until the age of eighty-four, when her boss passed away, and although she grows more compact and hunched by the year, she holds herself almost painfully erect, as if to show that true stature is an achievement.

Around behind the guardhouse stood my father. He too scrutinized the horizon, although facing in the opposite direction from my mother. "His new car," said Paul, nodding toward the haze-blue lozenge my father bought a week earlier. We stepped out, and my father lit up, shouting, "Elise! They're here!"

We continued the journey now in my father's car. Gateways held aloft the names of shtetls in Eastern Europe, and patchy earth rose and fell, undulating as we passed. The car started binging. "Are all the doors shut?" I asked.

"No, it's because I don't have my seat belt on," replied my father.

The binging turned quicker, more hysterical. "I don't buckle up always when I'm going slowly."

"It seems to make the car unhappy," I observed.

"Most accidents happen when a car is going under twenty miles an hour," said Paul.

My father drew the car over, and pulled the shoulder strap across his blue cotton windbreaker. The sun struck him as he straightened, illuminating a lean white-haired man of eighty-five who always dresses in trousers and a pressed shirt appropriate for an office even on the weekend. He'd been factory manager for an aerospace company in Manhattan for forty years, and still displays an engineer's precision. My siblings and I were trained to wear seatbelts and lock the front door with two locks, but lately, I've noticed, my parents just swing their apartment door shut, and even leave the window to the fire escape open at night, when once they locked it with a special octagonal bolt my father installed.

As I was leaving their apartment recently, they asked me to point to what I wanted to inherit. "I'll think about it," I replied. But they pressed me to say. I contemplated the decorative shelves beside the coat closet. "I like this goose-catcher," I said eventually of a Diogenes-like ivory figure, Chinese, holding aloft a basket to contain geese. "That?" said my father, as if he hadn't purchased it himself. "Why that? Do you want to know the most valuable item here? It's this," and he laid his hand on a vase of ruby rose. It was a saturating shade, a rose-petal tone that seemed to shimmy into the air around it. "Lalique," said my father. "Make a list of what you want," said my mother. I nodded but did not.

"The man who delivered you is here," remarked my mother. The arched entranceways were rolling by again, spelling out the names of old-world villages, many of the actual villages themselves already vanished. "Dr. Wachtel. Such a nice man."

"Busy here," said my father because the lane suddenly narrowed with parked cars. We stepped out onto surprisingly soft earth, which, after the city pavement, clasped our feet and gave a little, as if we were setting our heels into someone's palm. All the earth in the graveyard, in fact, was like that, unusually soft.

I strode under the sign for the village of Dokshitzer, hastening toward a familiar area. Paul grabbed my elbow. "Give them space," he said, and my face went hot as I realized I'd been brushing past people exiting as if I were going into Macy's. I nodded, and at that instant, as he passed me, one of the men glanced up. I was shocked to realize I knew him. Was he a relative? He was a modest, slouching fellow in a worn black suit. Ah, that's right, I remembered with a pang—he was an employee of the funeral home, Hirsch's. He was the watcher, the man who sat up all night with the deceased. My father saw him too, and nodded slowly in acknowledgment.

"Here's Miriam," called my mother. I hiked over, and studied the chiseled angles forming my relative's name. "She died young, of cancer," said my mother. "Miriam didn't get to get married. She was such a nice girl and she missed out on so much."

I nodded. There were certain things I longed for, still, and my mother's words reminded me of them. But I have an advantage over Miriam, I reassured myself—ashamed even at the moment of something unseemly in the thought. I'm still alive. "We'll come back to her," my mother said.

"Yes, *let's*," said my father emphatically, at her side now. "We should start with Anita."

The sound of my sister's name wrenched something inside me. We'd buried her less than a year before—my ears still heard the scrape of the gravediggers' shovels. The unveiling of the headstone had been in the spring, but my parents had gone by themselves, inviting no one.

We turned and began to search separately. The sun dropped layers over us, and the dust flung a kind of mica in the air.

Paul strode purposefully and I rushed from stone to stone, trying not to notice the names of relatives that weren't my sister. I kept recalling the upsetting conversation that Paul and I had had on Friday night. He wanted me to take a full-time job so he could retire someday soon. I'd felt ill at the idea of moving, and at something else having to do simply with how lost I seemed to be.

Something that I wanted was missing between us, yet I could not imagine leaving Paul. For days on end I'd forget about the thing that was missing, but then, despite myself, I'd remember it. Maybe a full-time job would transform me into a person who could leave or who could discover that she already had—or could create—what she wanted. And yet what if I just lost the otherwise sweet life with much writing time that I now had? I'd hardly slept Friday night, and then all day Saturday I'd worked on my curriculum vitae, and then on Saturday evening, since we had tickets, we went to the opera.

But even at the opera there was trouble. The man behind me kept rolling and unrolling the paper sheaf of his program. I glanced back and he didn't notice. I glowered and actually said "Shhh." He was a man of about seventy, I saw when I swiveled again. Paul caught my eye and frowned. "Don't focus on it," he murmured when the music swelled.

But still that man's hands kept up with their work!—twisting, untwisting, setting down with an air of finality, picking up an instant later. Finally, during one spectacularly exquisite passage I spun around, flying out of my seat, and my hand landed right on his. He leapt. "Stop doing that!" I said. And he did. Sublime silence, and the music even more beautiful than before. But then the paper shuffling resumed, he was getting his affairs in order, his hands had business that couldn't wait.

And the spoiled opera was on my mind at the graveyard, and my curriculum vitae which seemed impossible to complete according to the particularities of academia—I kept editing and rejiggering, I didn't know the official titles of all the adjunctships I'd had, and that very morning I'd had a conversation with an insider on a particular search committee which had made me realize again how ignorant I was of the workings of universities, how unlikely that my squirrely, insecure, hypersensitive, adjunctish personality could convince the academics on this search committee that I was the forthright Big Grown-up for whom they were looking—for, according to my acquaintance on the search committee, this was actually what they sought. I'd jotted her phrase. "A big grown-up," I said.

"Yes," she said. "A big grown-up. A grown-up grown-up. One with clout. The nonfiction department chair wants someone who will help him stand up to the fiction division. Someone comfortable throwing his or her weight around. A really big grown-up." My feet slipped on the soft earth. "There's Anita," I said.

"You found her?" my father shouted.

"Bonnie did," my mother called.

The new stone shone the color of soapy wool, clean-seeming, almost virginal, calling to mind a certain innocence that had clung to my sister. She'd passed away from multiple sclerosis a year before, at the age of fifty-one. Seeing the familiar shape of her name was like coming across her face. Her first name, capitalized, began and ended with a teepee, and possessed the tidiness that was characteristic of her person, a neatness like the snug triangular flap of an envelope or the tongue of a shoe that's been tightly laced.

Anomalously, when we were girls, Anita had carried a floral hankie, and when she sat reading from one of the enormous British novels she checked out of the library, and which were encased in brownish cellophane that crackled importantly, she sometimes rubbed the point tip of this hankie about on the inner rim of her nostrils. It gave her, she once confessed, a lovely feeling, as did her eating the Wise potato chips that she set upon her tongue while she read, drawing them from a bag hidden in the top of her desk—this delicate action, I sensed, providing a consoling contrast to the volcanic nature from which she suffered, the explosions of tears and venom, the eruptions of acne, the cascade of plaster dust from the ceiling when she heaved our bedroom door shut on our mother, who had merely inquired about the Weight Watchers meeting. Anita, beneath the grass.

My mother pulled out of a blue cloth tote printed YONKERS MUSIC SOCIETY a white bakery bag full of stones. She set four little rocks on the top of the headstone, each giving a tiny clack. "I brought enough to start a construction project!" she remarked. Then my father said, to my surprise, "I brought some prayers to say." He produced—from his pocket—glazed pamphlets printed in Hebrew.

"There used to be rabbis who roamed these places," he said, glancing around. Across the grounds the already-low sun struck the side of a tree trunk, rimming it with golden rust. A few last dark leaves pressed against the white sky.

"Yeah," I said. "There was one here years ago."

"Even last time there was one," he said emphatically, and I realized he meant when he was here with my mother in the spring. "Mom and I waited, and one showed up. There used to be a lot of them. Rabbis without synagogues. They'd be at the entrance or else wandering the paths looking for customers. And the customers would be looking for them!" He laughed, and I smiled.

His eyes continued to search. Swirled sunlight, ragged trees. A man in shiny black trousers and a rope belt had rushed over on a visit several years ago. "Need a bracha?" he asked, and my father nodded. He looked as if he lived on turnips and onions he yanked from the soil; his Hebrew was a dull drone from the old world. A rabbi without a congregation—or rather, with a congregation composed of mourners. A whiff of body odor came off him. I stepped back and he raised a bushy eyebrow in my direction, still chanting the prayers. He would say several words and then pause, letting my father follow him as if taking an oath. Once he pronounced a word a second time, emphasizing a syllable, and my father corrected himself. From girlhood I'd known only the rabbis of prosperous Riverdale, genteel, in Brooks Brothers suits. It had come as a revelation that someone could be a rabbi who didn't seem cerebral, partially abstracted into the empyrean already. My father and this man walked away from the graves after the rabbi sang a last psalm. Green flashed from palm to palm. My father spoke Yiddish and the man muttered Yiddish back, nodding. My father nodded, too. "Zei gezunt," said my father, but the graveyard rabbi had already tacked off and was almost halfway to the horizon. A knowledgeable acquaintance told me later that this man was likely not ordained, but merely an indigent luftmensch. Still my father remained sure such men were rabbis.

In any case, this man returned years later, in the person of the rabbi at Anita's hospital, a similarly uncouth fellow showing a rim of dingy undershirt. This man led the wheelchaired populace in the Friday evening services, his mustache a coarse salt-and-pepper that drooped into his wet mouth. And yet a few days before Anita passed away my father—preparing for the future, able to contend with it—visited this rabbi and not one of the Riverdale ones to ask him to perform her funeral. "He knew Anita," said my father.

"Did he?" I exclaimed. "You think so?" Was that Anita in the wheelchair? Toppled sideways, a paper towel around her throat at meals? Wasn't the real Anita the clever girl who'd gone downtown to Carnegie Hall to hear Alicia de Larrocha play Mozart?

"Sure," said my father. "At the end he knew her better than any of the Riverdale rabbis."

I lowered my head. This hospital rabbi had gone on to obey each rule as if each mattered—loudly counting out each time the coffin was set on the ground on the way to the burial site, checking and then double-checking to make sure there were the right number of men so all the prayers could be said. And this was, as it happened, exactly the service worthy of Anita, for whom God was as real as the tongue in her own mouth. Belief itself had always seemed the luck of the draw, to me. Anita and my father had it; my mother and I did not. My mother was a true *un*believer. For her, nothing supernal lurked behind the sagging russet velvet curtain of the ark, with its egg-yolk stitching and crown. Once I heard my mother ridicule my father's belief—he answered her in a soft, taut voice.

"I'm not saying I believe in an afterlife," my father said. "I don't. But I do believe in a creator. And I don't appreciate your mocking tone, Elise."

"I apologize," she said softly, and sipped her tea, an expression of incredulity still etched on her face, as if even her respect for him couldn't expunge it.

For me God was a rumor, hearsay, the opiate of the masses. And yet, as well, a shimmer at the edges of things. I myself was like someone who can't quite stop herself from believing in ghosts. She knows full well there's no such thing, and yet she can't quit being afraid. Such a person wants rabbis to be as cogent as professors, able to prove intellectually what must be true, their refinement itself an argument for the spirit world. They should not be like that graveyard rabbi with a rope belt, or the hospital rabbi with his stubble and warts.

"I remember the rabbis who roamed this place," I said to my father with a shrug. "Maybe they only come on holidays now."

"They used to be here all the time."

"Itinerant rabbis," murmured my mother, also looking away over the weather-beaten turf.

"A lot of them had been real rabbis in the old country. But they came here and didn't have congregations. And they didn't have other skills." My father peered at the battered landscape, and the sun slipped a notch, sliding behind an apartment building and taking with it the golden rim of rust. "Ah, well," he said. "No more."

He flapped the paper so that it was unwrinkled, sighed, bent his head, and began. He was not fluent in Hebrew, and the Hebrew he did possess had an archaic, clumsy bent. He said "Aw" where the clipped modern way was "Ah," and "beis" when schoolchildren now said "bet." His own father tore through the entire Haggadah impatiently as if he were muttering it all in God's ear, whereas the son balanced from word to word as if walking on seesaws. He wore black-framed glasses from the 1960s that over the decades had become surprisingly hip. My mother's slacks pooled over her black Reeboks. She especially seemed tiny, standing in the open air, the raw vastness all around.

And again, as with Anita's name, it was an experience of language and no language—the familiar percussive rhythm of the words, Yit'barakh v'yishtabach, time itself ticking, the white stones clacking from the sky, and I wondered when I would be saying these prayers for my parents, standing in the graveyard where they too had burial plots within sight of several three-story crumbling brick houses.

My parents probably had just walked by their own burial plots. I would have walked by mine and Paul's too, but I'd put off buying them. After I'd expressed interest, my mother had urged me two years ago to buy mine. She said, "They're going fast and there's hardly any room left there. This way, when people come to visit others in the family, it's easy for them to visit you too." But the paper with the particulars had migrated to a shelf in the kitchen with outdated coupons and warranties.

In fact, the woman I was supposed to contact, Esther Want, had apparently died herself. To my shock and horror, I'd seen her gravestone while looking for Anita. "Here's Mrs. Want!" I'd said to my mother, outraged. What right had she to pass away? I hadn't phoned her yet!

"Yes," my mother had said with a sigh. "Now someone else is taking care of this whole place."

But what would I do now, I wondered. Would I end up being buried in one of those enormous cemeteries beside the Long Island Expressway? Who would visit me? I would be so inconvenient! Why did I think there was no cost in letting one day melt into the next? I'd ignored in my own life what I really wanted—a more intimate relationship, to actually feel alive and present in my life—but it all seemed like something I could defer while I got my writing completed, while I composed my CV, while my entire being was like the hands of that man behind me at the State Theater, mechanically working something out while I also spun around and shushed myself, unable to immerse in the opera, and soon the opera would be complete. I seemed unable to be the grown-up grown-up that I needed and wanted to be. How to become that person?

"Let's find Mom now," said my father, referring to my mother's mother.

Again we prowled. At my grandmother's grave my father led us in the mourner's prayers, stumbling far less. Why, the ancient words only slightly clogged and jolted, now that he'd succeeded in praising God at the grave of his daughter.

My mother plucked some twigs out of the hedge of fir in front of her grave, and then we visited Aunt Bella and Morris. "He was so much fun, Morris!" remarked my father. I nodded, seeing that Jimmy Durante figure barreling away. "Yes, we have no bananas!" he'd sang, and I used to grin, half-wanting to look away from him out of burning shyness while at the same time thrilled to headachy ecstasy by his merry gaze which seemed to say, Ya see, ya see, isn't life grand? He nodded while he played, and smiled straight into my eyes. Why should I deserve this attention? I didn't believe I did. And yet he sang and played every time I visited, sitting me next to him on the bench.

"He could pick out any tune," I said to Paul. "I wish you'd met him."

"Able to light up a room," said my father. "What a lucky gift to have!"

"Aw, you light up a room, too, Dad, in your own way," I said. "And you too, Paul! And Mom!"

What a child! Having to reassure everyone.

My father smiled, and patted my hand. Everyone had been visited. It had taken about twenty minutes. The sun beat on our shoulders as we walked toward the road.

"We'll go to that diner, okay?" announced my father. "You remember where it is?" He glanced at his watch. "Twelve thirty. It's going to be a job getting parking."

* * *

Again we traveled past Jamaican bakeries and patty stands and storefront ministries. We followed my father, who drove slowly, perhaps not to lose us. "He drives like he's driving in the garage in his building!" said Paul.

I smiled. "Actually, though, you know, I like the way he drives."

Paul sighed. "I know."

The diner was indeed crowded. We were the only white people there, but my parents seemed oblivious. It was a vast place, half as long as a city block, and full of families in suits and dresses and glorious hats, coming from church. Over lunch we started talking about one of my parents' friends, Stan Grossman, who mumbled. He'd lost jobs in academia because his students couldn't hear him, and he became a scientist for the state. "A brilliant man," my father said.

"He investigated mice," said my mother.

"Their brains are actually similar to human brains," my father said.

"Your brother Ken spent a whole summer taking the brains out of mice," my mother said. "He thought he was going to learn a great deal from Stan Grossman but he didn't learn much. He couldn't hear him! He just took the brains out of mice all summer."

I laughed.

My mother shot me a glance. "You need to speak up in this life," she said.

The waitress poured coffee, and I told my parents about my job search. Suddenly my old bleary mood engulfed me, my fatigue from staying up late struggling with the CV, and with Paul's desire for me to get a full time job—anywhere, really—so he might retire and could quit shoveling his life into a corporation. He was in his late forties and had spent most of his life in an office, working long hours. Surely there was more for him.

My mother smiled at me across the table and took my hand. "Worry not, baby!" she said abruptly. "Worry not!"—words that always induce in me a feeling of acute concern.

"Okay, Ma," I said abruptly.

It surprised me that they didn't mind that I might be moving far away.

"I'm telling you, darling, and this is coming from a very old lady: It goes fast. Enjoy yourself. It's later than you think."

I smiled. What a crazy trick it was of my mother's, I thought—this guise of old lady, and yet she actually is an old lady. It's true she's the age of crones and fairy tale witches; she's shrunk now to only four foot eleven, and she's even acquired a slight curvature of the spine, the mildest hump—absurd of her, I think, as if I expect she can unstrap it, and stretch again, and be her tall vibrant self with the heap of russet hair, the young wife banging her shopping cart up and down the avenues of the Bronx or negligently letting the heel of her stiletto rasp against the pavement. She sleeps on her back now, with her mouth open. She even has a little wood cane the size of a vaudeville dancer's. She asked the shoemaker to cut it down for her. She took my hand now and kissed it. "Whatever you want, darling, you'll have," she said, half Tiresias, half Pollyanna. Or did she somehow really know my future?

"Have you made the list?" demanded my father, twirling a toothpick in his mouth as we stood on the pavement. He seemed to feel quite good. He rocked forward on his toes and then dropped his heels, as if his whole body felt light.

"I will," I said.

"Sweetheart, let's get this handled," said my father with novel determination. "It's time to quit putting it off. And remind me—there's something I want to show you when you come over again. A way to take down those decorative shelves near the coat closet.

There's a trick. You have to use a butter knife. Otherwise you'll rip half the plaster off the wall, detaching it."

My mother touched my arm. "We know you want the goose-catcher. But you have to tell us what else. Make your list today, as soon as you get home."

I smiled. "Okay," I said.

Then my parents drove off slowly in one direction and Paul and I sped off in another. I meant to call them later to make sure they'd made it home in one piece, but I forgot. I was busy working again on my CV, which had come to feel as impossible as a fairy-tale task, and then it all seemed like a fairy-tale task—trying to locate an ophthalmologist who could fix whatever was the matter with my mother's sight, trying to get my parents away from that horrible local dentist whose temporary teeth and bridgework always fell out.

Late that evening, the phone rang: "Have you written down what you want?" asked the tired voice. "Remember the red vase."

"It's on my list."

"Good!" she said. "Now we're getting somewhere!" She added: "But I'll believe your list when I see it."

I laughed. Frankly I don't want to accept my parents' gifts. I don't want to reach out my hand too quickly. I don't want to reach out my hand at all. And they know this and it pains them, as if they've given birth to a daughter who lacks the will to thrive, to press through the gates, to "open a mouth," as they say in the Bronx, to snatch up life as it should be snatched up—open your eyes, darling, get up, please, and walk!

In their own building, for years, lived their daughter Anita, whose movements grew ever more restricted. First came the cane, then the Amigo electric cart, then the wheelchair which others pushed. Still, one day my sister handed me a pen. She paid to have boxes of them made up, the only person I know who actually answered the offer to buy two boxes of personalized pens for just $19.95, and she gave them out to all her friends and acquaintances. "This is the day which the Lord hath made. We shall rejoice and be glad in it. Psalms 118:24," says the pen even though the ink has long run out.

The electric blue letters shine up from Anita's pen. I remember how her coffin was set down seven times on the way to her grave. And then a man appeared—the man in the tired black suit who I'd recognized that afternoon. He completed the quorum of men necessary so that the correct prayers could be said. He'd sat up with Anita after she passed away. He was supposed to chant psalms beside her all night long, and I believed from the look of him that he had.

He was a humble looking, slightly slouching fellow, this man who must be holy, mingling night and day with the spirits of the dead. My father tipped him but I kept staring, trying to see what he knew. But then, in the hugs and murmurings among the family afterwards, I lost track of him. I feel his presence sometimes, though. I glimpse him in the stranger on the subway who offers me his seat, and in the clerk at the bodega who, to my surprise, gives me some Asian persimmons he was saving for himself. Even in my sleep I am aware of him, like a boundary of the universe—a father's love, beyond which there is only arbitrary, interstellar dust.

"Goodbye darling," my father said, gazing down at Anita just before they shut the coffin. I didn't dare look at her in there, afraid of my own curiosity. My father closed the lid and withdrew, and the watcher slipped into the room behind us.

If the dead actually cross over a bridge, I think this humble watcher walks with them. I hope he does. I hope they don't have to cross alone. Because I've come to understand that dying feels like abandonment. If only we could have completed the fairy tale task! If only we could have fixed their teeth and eyes and all! Swept back the years with a stronger push of the broom. But we went off into our own lives—we had to. One evening I phoned my sister Anita in the hospital. She'd been in bed all day. This sometimes happened; the staff told me they lacked the pulley to hoist her from bed. The pulley was dirty, or on another floor. I called over to the nurse's station; I raised holy hell. And the pulley was produced from wherever it had been. But what haunts me is Anita's voice on the verge of tears: "I'm in bed. The others are all together. They're eating together in the dining room, and they left me in here."

Really, Anita? I thought. It really matters to you to be with that sorry crew? Those people with jaundice-yellow skin who must have their suppers spooned into their mouths? Those scarcely capable of conversation anymore, but who know you and nod, the man with just one leg, and the woman with plastic necklaces on her sunken chest—you want to be with them?

Yes. It matters altogether whether you are with them or not. What my sister taught me: Abandonment is torture.

Oh, if only the watcher could actually step into the spirit world! Walk right across the bridge with them when they have forgotten their identity and ours as well—reminding them, yes, you are not alone, I'm here. We want them to know that they were loved. We want to scrape off a piece of ourselves and send it, our own selves in the guise of this man so demure he's almost camouflaged. We send them a watcher and they send him back to us, a final gift, his eyes holding a humble, unearthly gaze from which it's hard to look away.

"Wake up! Wake up!" says my sister under the earth, a shattered temple of bone. "Wake up!" says my mother, bent under her bone hump. "I can't hear you," I cry, whirling about in my storm of papers, trying to vanish down the corridors of my prose. The old rabbis come after me, the ones with garlic on their breath, with dirt under their fingernails. "You were always a bad student," they say, accurately. "You learned to memorize; you learned to recite. But you never learned to think."

All true. I want to believe I am a character in a book, not a person alive on this earth. How to let oneself be alive, how to know it?—how to be a grown-up grown-up? My father visited the hospital rabbi, knowing his daughter would die any day. I wouldn't allow myself to know it. Even now I don't. A year or two after her death, she moved back in. She sits within me in her old apartment before the white box radio, listening to folk music. Similarly my ancient parents gaze down upon me with wizened eyes like the goose-catcher's, and I tell myself that I'll have them forever because they too have moved inside me, and that they'll never claim the land bought from Mrs. Want. What a child I still am!—needing to be told what things mean when the truth is chiseled in stone and I walked the too-soft earth myself, reading the inscriptions.

I finished the CV. It wasn't perfect, but it worked. I got a job. I moved. I wanted reality to rasp against me like the blades of a grater; I wanted it to shake me by the back of the neck like a dog with a rabbit in its teeth. How much easier—for certain of us—to be life's victim rather than to stand up and say, "This is what I want. And now I'm going to help myself." I used to tell myself, you're distorting, erratic, unable to take care of yourself. I populated my world with ogres, although I was told by the insider that it is desired that I be a grown-up grown-up. Why did I take so long to hear her? A grown-up grown-up is what I needed to be.

"Make your list," said my mother and at last I did. And I saw it was up to me to grant the wishes. My mother can't produce extra time from her hump—which is in fact the result of silent fractures, bone cracking under its own weight. How much more clearly could she show me?

My father, for his part, taught me to see the people from the other side—the psalm chanters, the shtetl shamans. Holy men, they commanded me to be unafraid, to leave my library, to take up my duties, to accept that we are bodies, fed on soil and made of sea, to titrate reality into me one risk at a time—making the phone calls, paying the bills, uttering the truths, hearing the grains falling in the glass—to run out and meet my life. You don't have infinite time to give to this one and that one, I learned at this job. If I surrender my time, I don't have it for what I need to do—the particular work which allows me to pay my own way.

Knowing I can leave makes staying sweeter. I am no longer beholden. My old dependence had made it impossible for me to challenge my husband. On weekends I made myself available for whatever expeditions he wanted—as if he were a fussy child who needed to be appeased. Paradoxically, experiencing my own strength has allowed me to see him as capable, quite able to create his own happiness. And beyond this—I discovered how convinced I used to be of my own ineptitude and of the world's essential brokenness. My despair over composing my CV had been, I came to realize, merely an instance of a permeating sense of the impossibility of things. Yet the more my job called me to do, the more instances I had to note that voice inside me screaming: "It will never work! You don't know what you're doing!" How could I be a grown-up grown-up when inside me a voice declared both my incompetence and the sad unworkability of everything?

I learned to ignore that voice. And over time I was able to hear in it a rote, impervious quality, as if it were a wind-up machine installed inside me. No wonder I'd felt half-alive for so long! I'd been saving up my life for tomorrow. I was the goose finally spied by the wizened Diogenes. I'd known all along I was a goose, I just hadn't known how to transmogrify, nor did I want anyone to know my secret: They were alive and I wasn't. I'd been afraid of the pain that becoming alive might cost, as if my husband and I would have to step through a sheet of plate glass to reach the living, as if life itself couldn't possibly be worth the price, which we might however pay when we were someone else, someone stronger and of greater means. At last I became that someone else, and I saw that I'd inhabited a trance, haunting a kind of graveyard of old ways that I finally managed to leave.

Late at night I hear, carried in the murmur of the wind, the voices of those who have gone away but who have sent me back a watcher, foretelling the end and the beginning of things. He stepped out of my own future; he had been waiting all this while. How faithless I was! What an idol I had made of security! I told myself actual happiness was an illusion, and so I never sought it. Yet as soon as I allowed change, what radiant glimpses I had of unknown watchers ahead! I passed over a bridge into a new life, and, looking back, I saw my old one was so narrow its sides almost touched.

THE MASQUERADE GUEST

I forbade myself to include that one episode. But that one episode, if I didn't include it, made everything else in the essay feel
emotionally false to me. I removed the affair from an essay about
keeping a writing notebook, and, in an instant, the essay went light
and hard as a meringue. I snipped it from "The Watcher," and,
at once, all that remained made no sense. What had been people
became cartoons; what had been of crucial, even sacred, importance became a game. And so I put it back. My secret insisted upon
itself. It held my writing life hostage. The affair—perhaps primarily
because it was a secret—seemed to be the point of contact between
my emotions and external reality. When I deleted it, I floated over
the earth, a humanoid spaceship. When I included it, I felt sad
and frightened.

Yet there was something misguided about this, for, in fact, the
essays held myriad truths that had nothing to do with the affair.
Still, the affair, if I didn't include it, seemed to deprive these essays
of dimensions, of validity. It occurred to me that my predicament
was like that of gay people who need to come out. I had an acquaintance who in fact came out to me twice, both times with great
emotion. The first time I'd been deeply moved. The second time,
as her voice trembled and she blew her nose, and her eyes avoided
mine but then peered straight at me, I had an impulse to laugh.
"You told me all this! You're gay!" I wanted to tell her.

But, embarrassed, I let her go through the process again, and hoped that this time it would stick and she'd remember she'd told me her reality. Now I could understand her compulsion to come out. A major secret demands that you communicate it or else the entire rest of your life feels fraudulent, even if it isn't. And essays, whose principle is investigation, most especially coax forth truth.

Yet why hurt my husband again? Must I really confess my worst behavior to anyone who plucked my writing off the shelf? My compromise was to include the episode, but in disguise. Here it was when I was thirty-four. And then here when I was forty-one. The disguise didn't matter to the veracity of the essay as long as I included the actual emotional impact of the event. It was the only untruth I introduced into the essays yet, ironically, it possessed the quality of restoring the felt truth value to things that were already valid. All the writer has to go on, however, is his or her felt sense of things, and so I couldn't forgo it.

My emblem stepped into the separate chambers of these essays wearing a Venetian harlequin mask. I've always liked that black half-mask that sweeps across the top of the face, held in place by an elastic thread. Here is a mouth: teasingly familiar, but not. Here is a frame of hair you recognize—but from whom? The bandit covers the bottom half of his face with a neckerchief; the masquerade guest covers the top with black-paper wings. Through many of my essays there stalked this guest, and at every point when he appeared I recognized my most alarming truth. He seemed to indicate something I was hiding from myself, and which necessitated my coming out to myself over and over again.

The facts are that I met him when I was forty-one. It lasted six months. My husband discovered. We talked about it. There had been reasons for why I'd felt my husband's absence so killingly that I'd been open to an affair. It was a relief to discover them. During the entire time I'd been lying, my husband had felt unreal to me. I recall the very day after the affair had begun, going to a concert with my husband, and all day long feeling that a wall of clear Plexiglas separated us. I kept waiting for the wall to go away. But when I woke up the next day it was still there. So his finding out was a terrible relief; it thinned the Plexiglas. And the conversations that followed thinned it further until it ceased to exist.

Yet the experience of having that affair continued to perplex. "I felt taken over. Driven. It didn't seem to be *me*," I once explained to a therapist. She nodded and calmly replied: "This is the most common experience of people who have an affair. It doesn't feel like it's them, doing it. The part of themselves they simply can't recognize is in control."

Still—how can it be that one element insists upon its admittance and holds the truth of the whole rest hostage—Septimus recalled in Mrs. Dalloway's party, the dark backing that lets the reflection spring into life? In my own case it was that I didn't believe in the importance of what had happened and so its importance was forced to insist upon itself time and again. It would not be rebuffed. It would not be forgotten. I had thought of myself as being almost infinitely plastic, as I believe many women do. One white lie can be spread beside the next until we've whited out our whole lives—but without actual cost to ourselves, we believe.

I didn't want to cause trouble. Nor did I believe that my life could accommodate the truth of what I'd experienced during that affair, and which I thought of as happening to a disqualified person, an incomprehensible person, the person who felt taken over, driven, painting herself with mascara, zipping up the snug skirt. All that seemed like something that had happened during an addiction or in a movie. It had nothing to do with me. This was the secret from myself that kept breaking forth. I did not actually believe in the reality of my own life. I thought it could be finessed. And so I had to keep admitting this florid token, this fetish, this signal of delirium, of irrationality—the unrecognizable aspect of myself that each essay tried afresh to introduce, to unmask and name.

In a Room Beside the Sea

"Hurry up!" shouted the cicadas.

The whole island rang with their celestial clamor, the thousand choirs of them sounding like innumerable stopwatches being wound in front of innumerable microphones, like maracas shaking.

"You're alive! You're alive!" they clattered at me. The place was famous for these chorusing insects, as it was famous for its honey, which Herodotus himself had acclaimed. But I knew of neither when I'd agreed to come. And I had work—work that had nothing to do with this place—that I desperately needed to complete. It was my tenure year. If I didn't publish a book, I would lose my job.

Still, who could turn down a month in Greece? An invitation like this had never come before. And so every morning I sat with the blue shutters latched closed, hunched in a darkened room beside the sea. There I tried to summon the Bronx, where my book was set. Discipline had always been my strong suit.

Yet I couldn't help hearing, through the air conditioning, the serenade of the cicadas, which grew louder and louder—at their peak they could rival a blowtorch—then, in an instant, fell to a stage whisper. Always, though, they maintained that distinctly upsetting urgency, which also possessed the rooster one town over who screamed his guts out: "It's day! It's day!", as if we were asleep while our houses were on fire. "Cock-a-doodle-do!" he screeched

149

all during the sunlit hours, not just at dawn, his hoarse voice on the verge of hysteria. "It's day!" Why didn't we hear?

But I did hear. Yet couldn't tell what it meant I should do.

Did it mean I ought to devote myself all day long to my manuscript, which was all that stood between me and being fired from a truly excellent job the likes of which I, at my age, and with this economy, would almost certainly never be offered again? Or did it mean I should get out and live, at least for a month, as if there was no tomorrow?

"You're *alive!*" came the maddening scream as I sat at my desk, and I shook my head, flummoxed, and every day felt I was living the day wrong.

At three I stepped out. Into an avalanche. The Greek sun flooded the white walls and floors, and carried the scent of the sea. I immediately felt like an idiot. All this was going on, and I was in my cave, playing with shadows. This is reality, the sunlight seemed to say. Look! It was a radiance purer than any light I'd seen—purer than the sheen of Florida, the stark, caliper-precise air of Maine. It was a rinsing, brimming, yet factual light, as if it was taking into account every molecule of material existence and ecstatically acknowledging it. And I could have been out in it, enjoying it, enjoying Greece.

One afternoon when I stepped out, I saw that the apples on the spindly tree opposite my door had grown. Could it be? We'd been there just two weeks. Still, they were the size of bottle caps when we first came. Now they were big as flashlight lenses. Also, the black kitten, who had at first been the size of a suitcase handle, was also bigger, visibly so, even in those rushing weeks. Only the honeysuckle blossoms were unaltering, and the bulky grandmother in her long dress who sat outside on a chair, smiling, saying "*Kalimera*" as if she thought I could understand.

In the Bronx, where I grew up, I'd never seen things grow. The tree leaves would be big. At another time they would be tiny, or gone. Now each afternoon I stared at the apples when I opened the door, and my eyes searched out the black kitten, which the bulky grandmother fed as if he were a chicken—a scattering of kibble on the flagstones. If we came back next year (we should be so lucky) would he remember us—although I secretly fed him tidbits each night, and he came running now whenever he saw me? In a year, would the cat we loved have vanished, subsumed into a bland black cat of ordinary size and girth? An odd sentiment possessed me as I walked across the courtyard, and I felt that it would be entirely reasonable to devote the next two weeks to simply staring at this cat while he grew.

I met my husband at the café that had Wi-Fi. "Let's go!" I said. We often visited abandoned hilltop towns in which medieval stone walls had toppled in. Dried grasses and mosses flourished here. And the rattle of the cicadas was, if possible, even louder. Then we found our way to a beach, a different one almost every day of that month, and plunged into the ever-moving sea.

Even the sea had changed during the course of these two weeks, growing warmer, easier to slip into, ever more beckoning. At night we ate tomato salad and drank the white wine sold everywhere on the island, and dark fell as fast as a yanked curtain. "Beware the quick fall of night," advised a local walk book. The gigantic sunlit hours were beguiling, dangerous, promising to last much longer than they in fact did. Hiking in the countryside, one could easily be stranded in the wilds, in the dark. We eyed the sun warily whenever we set out on foot during the shimmering afternoons.

By the time I lay in bed at night, exhausted, I had the feeling I'd accomplished a very great deal simply from having swum and smelled and seen, despite the fact that the Bronx book wasn't going particularly well. It was about my parents, and somehow I couldn't figure out the right ratio of scene to introspection; the proportions were always off. By bedtime, though, a feeling of well-being pervaded. The moon one night was the precise saffron color of the sheen inside the honeydew melons that grew on the island. It was enormous, swollen in the sky. And then, a few nights later, it was a wisp. I felt that I was understanding the message of the cicadas at a different level than the level of thought although I couldn't yet say what it was. At some point during the night, though, I became a girl strapped to a plank headed quickly toward the tenure buzz saw. How it whined in my ears! When I woke up I realized I was hearing the cicadas singing.

At the start of the third week, though, something shifted. I realized that if I didn't write down what had happened the day before, I began to lose it. In a few days, its details would be gone.

And so I began my workday noting the day before: the tiny white church of Agia Sofia erected inside a cave high in the mountainside, its gold-encrusted paintings flaring as you blinked in the humid darkness, stepping out of the leafy woods and into the mouth of the cave; a single bat winged overhead, and the ikons stared with enormous, commanding, compassionate eyes that seemed to see through layers and layers to your very depth. The mountain pool we swam in, where, nearby, spiders hung in the vacant air, their giant webs quivering into visibility only at the instant the spider flexed. The Athenian man with the urbane, curlicue beard who ran the concession booth at Lagada beach, and who showed us his garden, encouraging us to inhale the aroma of the tomatoes, "even though they are green! You see?" he demanded, as if the goodness of life were implicit in that scent.

All this I wrote, and other things besides, until it became obvious that Greece was driving out the Bronx. Every day there was more Greece, less Bronx. Some days there was no Bronx at all. "You are ruining your life!" some part of me screamed, desperate as those cicadas. "You need to be working on your Bronx book!"

"I refuse to lose this life experience. I accept the consequences," the rest of me replied at once, a trifle glibly, for I was afraid even though I'd made my choice.

I was seeing what I never had—no, I was feeling what I never had: that the body and the mind are not separate things. Some lines from Kazantzakis came to me: "I should fill my soul with flesh. I should fill my flesh with soul." Yes, I felt—now I understood what he meant. And I could also see that, quarantined from the experiences of the body, the mind becomes arid—and prone to self-deception and bewildering self-doubt. What circles I was walking in, in my Bronx book!

I'd always lived as if temporal things were of secondary importance: the haziness or glitter of the stars, the precise taste of cherries on my tongue, or my ninety-one-year-old mother's voice on the phone (for I called her just twice, for a few minutes, in all that month), exclaiming, "Oh, I love you! I love you!" over and over. What a fool I was. My entire Bronx book could be no more eloquent than that! Why had I made it so very complicated?

The final week brought another change. I quit the writing desk at noon, leaping up, eager to get going. At dusk that last week, after a blazing day, I came upon a bulky figure rinsing herself off with a hose toward the back of the property. It was the old grandmother. There she stood in her one-piece, her hair streaming. She'd gone swimming in the sea. She gave me a radiant smile that I could hardly return, I was so moved. She'd gone swimming. She'd gone swimming. It was as if my own sister, immobilized by MS for many years, had actually gotten up and enjoyed. It was as if to say that all those we think lost to happiness still have a chance—and they will snatch it.

This was more beautiful than the kitten scarfing up the scraps of silvery fish I'd brought him, more beautiful even than the brimming moon itself, completing its grand, stately procession across the dark sky.

I was happy for the first time in years, I realized. All the tenure-track writing, with its endless second-guessing, had filled me with misery. But now a sense of peace and happiness welled up. Greece was giving me what I hadn't known I lacked. I simply wrote what had happened the day before and its significance seemed to stream through it without my having to go searching. And a certain loneliness that had haunted me for years, I noticed, had vanished.

I was aware that the Lotus Eaters were natives of Greece, their story conveying the lure of these exquisite islands. Still, all that last week I fed myself on the native honey. Who cared if I developed a craving for it, and couldn't obtain it once home? Today, today, sang the cicadas, and I sang it too. Here was the very honey praised by Herodotus, its flavor due to the wild thyme that grows on the mountaintops. I was tasting what he'd tasted! It had a sequence of flavors: first rum, then a blaze of sweetness, then an herbal note. And the jar glowed like a lantern as I wrote, for I'd opened the shutters at last.

"All exotic places are alike," said the man who ran the local gym. Perhaps they convey to the visitor the secret message that he or she most wants to hear.

Mine had to do with discovering that I was part of life itself. I'd shut the door against that knowledge years earlier. But now I saw with my own eyes that things really grew, and so, it followed, they must perish. This too was okay, although I'd shut my door years earlier precisely so I would never discover this. The cat, growing so quickly, the apples, the tomatoes, all were attached to the vine of life itself, as was I, as were all whom I loved, including my parents in the Bronx, whose death seemed the worst thing I could endure. No wonder I was writing a book about them. I wanted to fit them into a book and have them forever. But I was reassured now from having seen the cycle of life, or rather, having felt its pleasures in my body. Somehow I could consent to it now, this thing from which I'd sequestered myself away.

The value of life *is* life, I suddenly felt. For the first time I really understood that we aren't here just to do a job, but, as the sages have often told us, also to be. Darkness falls fast, after all. I recalled the enormous eyes in the cave, gazing outward, waiting to rendezvous with the traveler who sets foot from the glare of day into the shadowy dark. I see those eyes even now, gazing and gazing at the beauty before them, the growing leaves at the mouth of the cave, the little bat, wheeling, the solitary traveler who, tired, worrying about the failing light, finally steps into the sacred darkness and finds him- or herself met by a compassionate, intimate gaze, as if nature itself were saying at every point, Don't worry, you are not alone, I am one with you, you are part of the infinite, there is hope for you yet.

BEYOND COMPARISON

We were leaving tomorrow but I had little desire for home. I sipped the cheap white wine whose dry tang cut pleasantly through the richness of the grilled sardines, and glanced up at the fig leaves spread over us in the courtyard. My life in the States seemed one tangle of tensions and worries. If only there were a way to bring home this serenity! For I felt, at the moment, such a penetrating sense of well-being from a month exploring the countryside on this Greek island that it was as if I'd experienced an epiphany and had been permanently altered—as I wished I had been. Well, I *had* experienced an epiphany, but once home, I suspected, the old anxieties would creep back.

Just then a hectoring clamor burst out. A voice being broadcast by a microphone echoed through the winding streets. It had a hortatory, urgent, demagogic tone. The proprietress drifted out onto the flagstones. A few children on bicycles rode up.

"What is it?" my husband asked the proprietress, who spoke English. "Something to do with the economic crisis? A political candidate?"

She inclined her head and regarded us, her eyeliner imbuing her gaze with a certain antique hauteur.

"The announcement—" pressed my husband.

"Ah!" her expression brightened. "This is a chicken truck."

"They're selling chickens?" I exclaimed.

"Exactly."

I laughed, relieved. And pictured the cellophane-wrapped packages in my local Key Food. Yes, it must be inconvenient for housewives in this hilltop village to get to the market. And then it occurred to me: "Are the chickens live?"

"Of course."

A few moments later, from out of the gathering dusk there materialized a lumbering blue truck. It was a tall, canvas-topped, tippy-looking vehicle that consumed almost the entire narrow street. And sure enough, when I stepped behind it, there they were, chickens, shifting about in stacks and stacks of crowded cages towering to the very roof. The chickens were so pale they looked naked—the white bodies soft, pliant, disturbingly unguarded. There were also beautifully shaped ducks, at the very back near us, gazing with cheerful, curious eyes. An unshaven young man stood beside the truck, clasping a boxy microphone close to his mouth, and that demanding metallic voice banged off the walls. No buyers appeared, though, and, after ten minutes the truck began to roll away. Paul jostled me. "Look!" A word was emblazoned across the back of the truck in metal letters. METAPHOR, it said in Greek.

I laughed, bewildered. "Why would you put that on your truck?"

"Strange," Paul agreed.

A peculiar note had been added to our evening, although it was one I'd experienced before during our visit here—a sensation of the supersaturated significance of things. I'd been, years earlier, to France and to Italy—both sumptuously beautiful, and yet neither imparted this feeling of the overdetermined meaning of events and objects. I'd felt it for the first time three weeks earlier, happening upon a mosaic of Dionysus. The god glanced out with knife-bright, presumptuous eyes, fresh vine leaves twisted in his hair, and a wry secret clasped between smiling, shut lips. I understood, with a shock to my bones, that people had actually truly believed in Dionysus. And for days after it had seemed to me that that particular god hovered so near I could feel his body heat.

On another occasion, perhaps a week after that, we'd been invited to dive into an underwater passage where you could swim twelve feet, holding your breath, and then emerge in a cove where seal pups lay. A friend of ours had done just this, vanishing under the mountain and rushing through the dark, then breaking the surface in a cavern where he could breathe freely. His wife, who stayed behind with us in the boat with their toddler, cursed her husband until he reappeared, grinning. "You should do it!" his voice rang out. "Do it now!"

We all refused. And yet that cavern hollowed by the sea had sounded familiar. As we stood on the boat awaiting the husband's return, I realized that I'd read about it. It was the place in *The Odyssey* where the adventurer hides among seals in order to grab Proteus and make him tell his secrets. Proteus changes shape time and again. Odysseus clasps a lion, a snake, a leopard, a boar, mere water, a tall tree and at last the old man himself—"the Ancient," as Fitzgerald calls him—who reveals the news from home. The entire time the husband was gone under the mountain I contemplated this—the realization that sometimes you need to hold on through all a god's changes.

Finally, one last instance of this jarring sensation of significance occurred when my husband and I climbed up a wooded cliffside and came to a cave in which a little white church had been erected. Agia Sofia. It was a one-room plaster edifice, this church, but even as you paused in the mouth of the cave, getting your bearings, the scent of loam and decaying earth rising up around you and a bat wheeling in the air, your eyes glimpsed canvases of gold. One entire wall of the church—the one facing the cave entrance—was covered with gold-leaf paintings. They presented Byzantine figures, with the canvases hung low so that their enormous, kind, painted eyes peered straight over the brief front wall of the church at—and seemingly into—the visitor.

Those eyes. The artists had put all they knew of humanity into them. You are okay, you are okay, they implied, the sacred heads tilted, their folded gowns rigid as cathedral reticulations. It came to me, inhaling the dank earth, that the earliest sacred spaces were caves, and so this place was perhaps a chapel within a chapel. Did that account for its echoing force? Or was it simply the gratuitously compassionate gaze of those ikons, which looked at me for days after, until my very depths felt illuminated and their rigid poses were as familiar as those of the mournful, majestic kings on playing cards. If I never stepped into that cave again (and I almost certainly never would), I felt I would carry those figures with me.

Now my husband and I returned to our table and finished our supper under the vine leaves—savoring the local watermelon, the baklava so fresh it wasn't like any I'd tasted in the States. Instead of desiccated leaves and hard, stale honey, this dripped. Our mouths were soaked. From time to time a clamor reached us—the exhortations of the chicken truck reverberating far across the countryside—and we smiled. Our old friend! Still, beneath my pleasure, I felt heartsick. I'd experienced something crucial here. But since I couldn't identify what it was, I would lose it, I felt, the way you can lose an important dream.

To delay our return, my husband and I wandered the twilight town. It was one of those semi-deserted places one found high in the interior. Three children played kickball in a dusty playground. There was absolutely no automobile traffic. Eventually we encountered a woman trailing behind a muddy dog, and, a long time later, an old rigid man with a walking stick, progressing as if his bones ached. In a ramshackle yard, a ram with a scraggly white beard and horns jabbed into a little lamb that was trying to get near the food. Suddenly our pathway was lit: "METAPHOR" read the sign in the front of the truck as it careened silently past.

Paul burst out laughing. "This all sounds like a dream you'd tell in therapy."

"I know!" I exclaimed. "But what does it mean?"

As it turned out, we had ample time to contemplate that an hour later, when we found ourselves on a dark, winding road wedged behind the creeping chicken bus. A brilliant lightbulb illuminated its interior. The good part about riding behind this circus truck is that we traveled safely along the treacherous roads as if behind a snowplow in a storm. But mile after gradual mile held suspended before us this vision of the rattling towers of pale chickens, the ducks with their eager dark eyes and their bodies like yin-yang waves, and above it all the blistering bare lightbulb shedding radiance.

Was the meaning: Don't be a victim? Or: we are all simply caged beasts making our way across the countryside to our doom!? Or just: you are right to avoid eating meat? Or even—and suddenly this seemed equally true—life will present absurd visions; God too is an artist, with his own creative unconscious. You can't understand everything.

And all this while, within me ranged that other, more urgent question: how could I bring home the sense of well-being? For I'd been happy—life had felt really worth living, actually—for the first time in several years. I glanced at my husband, relaxed behind the wheel. The radio played folk music, half-gypsy, nasal, intricate, the melody braiding. The country lay dark on either side. What a beautiful ache the singer put into his voice, as if the loss he was singing about held such a great life truth that it gave him happiness. The idea possessed me that I could find what I was searching for if I examined that very afternoon, from which my bathing suit was still damp. If I could seize its still-near form, I'd discover the divinity that was hidden by all the shape-shifting.

That afternoon I'd swum for the very first time in a mountain pond beneath a waterfall. It was the most freezing water I'd ever entered, and it had terrified me. Would it induce a heart attack? The water in the pond shone a brilliant green, the jade of a mineral-stained tub. A Greek myth told about a woman smitten by love of a river god, I'd suddenly recalled. The pulses in my wrist and throat throbbed as I paddled up to the waterfall and back, gasping. Paul sat with his hands clasped on his knee in an underwater chair created by a web of tree roots. He'd somehow acclimated to the impossible element. He was a Beardsley dwarf from the chest down, but with a humane, handsome, bemused, regular-sized face.

Splash!: a frog had leapt in. And, near my toe, when I stepped forward, a leaf shard the size of my pinky nail drifted back. But—could it be?—as I looked, the leaf shard revealed itself to be a crab. Yes, it was a tiny crab—a complete, entire, alive creature. For an instant I had the kaleidoscopic feeling that there were tiers of life from entities the size of mountain ranges to beings so infinitesimal that people never detected them. And I was just another creature among them. I felt *okay*, part of things, at home in the world, no longer comparing myself to this one or that one, amidst the beauty of this place.

Immersed, it occurred to me that life in my college town made me feel disconnected. Isolated. Curtains drawn, I hunched in my study all morning and taught in a university in the afternoon and evening, and the entire time I was racing the tenure clock, and other clocks too: the one marking my ninety-one-year-old parents' lives in the Bronx, the one that ticked off the lives of friends in the east while I was in Texas, the one that told me how many minutes I had for my writing before I needed to start grading papers for the day's teaching, and all the while inside me a White Rabbit chanted: "I'm late!"

In Greece, though, the race ceased. I didn't check Facebook. I didn't open e-mails. I recalled Elizabeth Bishop living in Brazil, foregoing constant comparison with others in the U.S. literary world, transporting herself away from envy, grandiosity, and maybe even that third step in the waltz, depression.

As my husband and I walked back beside the creek, having climbed up above the waterfall, I noticed a brackish area where the current didn't move. A dozen darning needles lay in the air, attached to tall grasses, absolutely parallel to the water as if set on an invisible current, their neon blue horizontal pennants glowing. "Look," I said to Paul. He tossed a glance but kept on. I lingered, though, staring at the evidence that even still places have their loveliness. Higher up that hillside, when we entered the realm of the sun, we saw Queen Anne's lace that had dried in the blazing light, attaining a stark, enduring beauty. Wasn't there some way I could bring back this happiness, I'd wondered—this sense of being beyond the snare trap of comparisons?

For—I suddenly admitted to myself, gazing into the chicken truck—during the time I'd had my tenure track job I'd become increasingly aware of being ordinary, even as I was also distinctive. My job required that I submit my writing frequently, and so I was exposed to more rejection, even as I received many acceptances. "Rejection is your friend," chanted a colleague who'd won a prestigious fellowship the fourth time he'd applied. Some days I chanted that, too. At other times, though, I felt no smarter than anyone else, no more perceptive than anyone else, no more fun than anyone else. In some very basic sense, I was quite ordinary—and this actually had an air of liberation in it. But now, suddenly, it occurred to me that the grid of comparisons was itself the illusion.

I lifted my gaze from the word METAPHOR, and stared again at the webwork of glittering wire, and I saw myself as one of the chickens with fevered eyes peering at the impossible rigid web. Paul drove calmly on. The gypsy singer on the radio, raspy-voiced, nasal, was delivering a tale that wrenched his heart and nevertheless filled him with a great life joy. You hear how it is? You hear how it is? he seemed to ask. When we finally reached our apartment, I sat out on the little deck and watched the silvery hammocks of the sea, and the moon, stately, pristine, perched impossibly far above us yet pulling at the waves.

"'Metaphor,' in both ancient and modern Greek, means to transport," I read early the next morning, sitting back out on the deck in the sunshine.

My mouth let out a gasp. What?! There was no fancy significance? It was merely a truck advertising brand: Transportation? Like U-Haul? I smiled, shaking my head, and saved this up to tell Paul, who was still in bed.

And yet I marveled at discovering the meaning hidden in the familiar term. Yes, of course: metaphors transport. You fly for an instant to a reality where you're shown truth in a new, more telling guise.

Still, I thought, wryly disappointed, thinking of the squalid chicken truck into which I'd peered and peered as into a holy ark—how very typical of me to search for something ultimate. Transportation! Ha! The sea winked and shimmied below me. A thousand pinpoints flared. Angry at myself, I widened my eyes and let the burning, shifting surface fill my gaze. My eyes itched and then began to blaze, but I wouldn't blink.

How I'd craved a secret meaning to bring home. Something that would save me from reverting back to my old, struggling life. But metaphor was just the truck brand. That's all my vision meant.

Eyes on fire, I tried to stare an instant more, another instant, until my mistake was burned away, until I was someone else, someone more intelligent, but the lids clapped shut of their own accord and then I couldn't stop blinking. In the serene cove, old people slowly strolled in twos and threes, chatting, the cool water lapping their shoulders. They loved the early hours.

Back in Texas I had been trying to establish something about myself, to achieve. My body became an inconvenience. I lugged it from place to place, clad it, blow-dried its hair, buttoned it into professional cotton-poly shirts, and then I set it before my students, where it began a kind of anxious performance. Only hours later, as I was walking at night up the quiet pavement, did I return to myself. And then, if a student exclaimed, "Professor Friedman!" I was surprised—that I was known, after all. It startled me that I could be *seen* when I wasn't actually putting on The Bonnie Show— an old sensation, as if to be visible required some special shiny *effort*. And yet this effort itself ensured that whatever attention I received seemed intended for that glittering metallic construct, my personality.

But in Greece, that was altered. The body here wasn't just the compartment in which I lived. It had its own value, and, strange to say, identity. It was accepted by the sun, the water. And it received gifts. There was the kindness of the honey to one's tongue, and the kindness of the warm sun to one's skin. A line from Emerson returned to me: "These roses on my windowsill make no reference to former roses or to better ones; they are for what they are; they exist with God to-day."

And, now that I thought about it, how many gifts I'd received even early on in the Bronx, before I'd proved anything, before I'd accomplished. The Bronx had been filled with gifts. There'd been the splayed green keys of the polynoses on the pavement of Harrison Avenue that my sister pointed out. And my father's wingtip shoes running up the avenue as he held on tight to my bicycle—and then took his hand away but still hurried, letting me discover for myself I now knew how to ride a bike. Gratuitous gifts! Not given because I was of use. *I was not of use!* And nevertheless I'd been deemed fit to receive them.

So why had I become so desperate to prove myself? The harder I tried to establish some special quality, the more ordinary I'd felt, and the more I had the sensation that what I had inside was actually shameful.

I nodded, looking at the cove of early morning bathers. Yes, finally—finally!—I was approaching something I could bring home, a hint about how not to get ensnared in my old way. Connect with the realm that is beyond better-than and worse-than, I told myself. It is here, always available in the present instant. The present moment is beyond better than and worse than. The sublime isn't what's distant.

My finger tapped the dictionary. If only—I used to think, staring at the constellations in the dark heavens that my sister traced with a raised finger—if only I could understand the ideas lurking behind things, then all the tensions of life would cease. My parents would no longer be getting older, and my grandmother wouldn't seem so sad, and I myself would feel less uncomfortable in my own skin—if only I could understand the hidden meaning!

Yes, long before the concerns of tenure, I'd assumed that my own life was merely a metaphor for something else, an antechamber to a more important life where the hidden meanings stood revealed. How I'd discounted the reality of the body and the senses; how otherworldly I'd always been! But the metaphor truck said: This is it. This is what's real. Simply the chickens rattling in their cages. Simply the ducks with their dark, blistering eyes.

For a moment, before it hid itself away, I sensed the identity hidden by the shape-shifting. This *is* real. Your life is real. A god already lurks within. You are ordinary and extraordinary, at once. There's nothing that needs to be forced.

Below me on the street a man was selling tomatoes from the basket of his bicycle. An elderly Greek woman, my neighbor, bargained with him. The moon was a faint chalk shore in the sky. I nodded, looking at the old Greek people immersed up to their shoulders in the shimmering water, most of them wearing hats, strolling about as if in a plaza. And got up to pack my suitcase.

The Vagabond Queen
of Craig's List

I wept when my husband and I had to give up our apartment in Brooklyn so I could go off and teach at the U. of North Texas. My landlady simply would not let me sublet. "I'll pay a year up front!" I pled. (So what if it risked my savings?) "I'll let you approve the subletter!" (Surely we could find somebody on whom we both agreed.) It frightened me to have no home in the city in which I'd grown up—as if I'd become a stranger to myself. But the landlady was adamant: *No, no,* and *no.* She needed direct control of who lived in her apartments.

All that final summer I walked around the neighborhood morose. Goodbye, fruit market on Atlantic Avenue, where sunset-orange mango chunks and beds of ruby pomegranate seeds gleamed, raising my spirits on difficult days. Two of my literary heroes had written about this roaring, ragtag thoroughfare. Frank McCourt lived for a year right over Montero's Bar after his first marriage broke up. He'd both hated and loved the place. His apartment pulsed with music and seemed a shameful spot for a schoolteacher to live in, but the bar did have its charms: one need never be alone. And here was Montero's still, with its creaking blue neon sign, its dusky interior.

And the nature writer Edward Abbey, on the very first page of *Desert Solitaire,* talked about the docks at the end of Atlantic

Avenue. The fact that two of my favorite authors had referenced a street in my neighborhood made me feel a covert affinity with them, a secret strength—if they could find success despite real limitations, so could I. Oh, I did not want to give up this place! I was a mess that August day when the movers hauled my possessions down the stairs.

"But you can sublet places on Craig's List!" said my friend Sally, during our goodbye supper. "Sample other parts of the city during winter and summer break! It'll be an adventure."

I sighed. What a Pollyanna! Didn't she understand it was change itself I most disliked?

Yet Sally was right. For the past four years I've been the vagabond queen of Craigslist.com, hopscotching Brooklyn. And the adventure has been wonderful. While I live in each apartment, I study what it has to teach. I read its books, eat the food on its shelves, and consider the perspective from its windows.

Beyond that, I've been forced to undergo a spiritual education in acquiring and then letting go. It's as if I were a hermit crab inhabiting one distinctive shell after another, or a reincarnate who got to live through many life cycles while being allowed to keep her memory of each.

And something has shifted in me, thanks to this reiteration of loss and gain. I've begun to internalize that this is just the way of things: alteration, change. The tide washes in innumerable things— some marvelous, some mere hard grit—then sweeps them forth. Again. Again.

I appreciate with keener delight and observe more closely each fresh place. And when it's time to return the key, it's with a more transitory sense of regret, an almost bemused sense of the lightness of being. How often I've emptied drawers of my possessions! Why act as if my happiness is suffused in these walls, interfolded with these books, dependent on the chirp of the particular bird who nests in this tree? Of course some part of me still believes that my happiness *is* all these things, totally synonymous with each place. But another part of me—brand new, marveling, even kind—gazes on and says, *Yes, yes, of course. Get teary, if you must! But haven't you learned by now, you naïf, the gift of this experience? Ah, yes: you see it for a moment, then lose track of it again!*

I nod to myself, blowing my nose, and do my best to fix my gaze out the cab's front window, instead of at the receding image of my last temporary residence.

My first winter break I found an apartment in Red Hook, near the Columbia waterfront—a loft owned by a graphic artist with a truly lovely eye. There was a Parisian kitchen with black-and-white floor tile and dangling copper pots, and a living room with dozens of seriously flourishing plants—a source of worry since houseplants tend to wither under my care. I took pages of notes on when to water and learned to assess soil with my fingertips and to notice the precise tinge of leaves. My first morning in that sequestered apartment I woke up and lay in bed, astonished. Opulent silence enfolded me, luscious as mink. Who knew the city could be this serene?

I'd always lived in apartments that were more centrally located and that carried the city's clang; one of them even jounced up and down like an elevator with each passing truck. I had no idea the city also had such pockets of silence.

The Red Hook artist's space was so pretty that I was inspired to keep it neat, and that, in turn led me to host a dinner party. I invited friends for New Year's and ordered trays of pasta and chicken from Cucina Napoletana. My friends had never been inside any apartment with my name on the lease; I'm so messy that no one's allowed in. Yet now I discovered the pleasure of trying to give a beautiful evening to friends.

The shelves in that first apartment held a book with photos of Stanley Kunitz's garden, accompanied by his poems. I read and reread the poems and gazed at the cobalt-blue irises and sheaves of lavender. The flowers rose out of soil that Kunitz had created himself from years of mulching seaweed.

After decades of reading only prose, the rediscovery of the concision of poetry. And after a lifetime of asphalt, the revelation that soil itself is something you can grow.

Gin stood poised on a high shelf in the kitchen of this apartment. If I couldn't sleep, I stood on a chair and fetched the Beefeater's, adding tonic water from the icy fridge. Yum. And then: blotto—a velvet sledgehammer delivered me into blank unconsciousness. I rarely drank gin. But the entire time I was in that apartment I allowed myself, if I woke up during the night, to sip. And eat the crystallized ginger in the Mason jar. I was Goldilocks. What fun to try out everything.

The very last day, I replaced what I'd taken, and a hollow sadness shook me. I looked out the rear cab window, confused by loss all over again, as the driver took me to LaGuardia. It didn't matter that I'd known from the outset my stay was temporary.

And yet I was starting to see that the city itself brimmed with hidden treasures, and that my clinging to what I'd known had prohibited me from finding something better.

That summer I rented in Fort Greene, also from a graphic designer. She was a slight person who lived without one comfortable piece of furniture. The chairs were hard plastic, the sofa an Ikea cushion on wood ribs. But I loved walking around and around Fort Greene Park for exercise, the gigantic old trees blossoming.

My husband bought a handmade fedora at Malchijah Hats. Changing the hatband, if you ever wanted to, came free.

"You doing it! You doing it!" exclaimed a man on the street—smiling at my husband's hipster style, but not nastily.

The night before we departed that second apartment I sat on the brownstone's steps. All my senses were heightened. Such hushed, leafy streets! The jingling chain of a dog; the whistle of a man, strolling. I was stricken again with melancholy. Saying goodbye was both easier than before and just as hard. It's unfair, I protested with childish logic: *I love this, therefore I should get to keep it.* And yet despite myself, the city was teaching me that those treasures I most enjoyed were the ones I could least anticipate because they were devised by people whose personalities had different strengths than mine.

I was learning, too, that surprise was crucial in determining what I might fall in love with. The world was often better than I expected. I didn't have to be so in control all the time, so on guard. Why, even something tiny can cause great pleasure! I recalled the Fort Greene neighbor who wore around her neck a bandana out of which one day poked a brilliant yellow triangle that cried, "Peep! Peep!" "Is that a bird around your neck?" I asked. It was. It had fallen out of its nest, and this woman was nursing it to health. She'd worn it everywhere: on the subway, on her dog-walking jaunts. She showed it to me, opening her bandana further: the plump black glossy grackle body, the gleaming eye above the urgent yellow beak. *See*, I told myself. *You never know what beautiful surprise might come!* Stay put, and you see less. And that thought provided some balm as, next morning, I hauled my suitcase down the stairs.

The third apartment we rented from a composer on Middagh, in Brooklyn Heights. It was a famous, tiny street. Carson McCullers had lived here with both Auden and Gypsy Rose Lee while Gypsy wrote *The G-String Murders*, although their house itself was long ago sacrificed to the BQE. Around the corner from our new digs was an Egyptian cafe where for $4.50 you could get falafel with pita they cooked on the spot. You ordered, and the man rolled out the dough with a rolling pin. Down the hill was the new Brooklyn Bridge Park, where I found myself standing beside Mayor Bloomberg at a food-film festival. I'd had a glass of beer at the festival, and now the mayor manifested himself. "We love you, Mayor Bloomberg," came the voice out of my pleasantly inebriated self. "You're doing a wonderful job!" How deeply tan he looked, as if he'd just arrived from the Bahamas. "Wha'd I do?" he asked, with comic modesty. I said nothing in response, for I had reached the end of my euphoric ability to hobnob with the famous.

Or had I? Because, although he was instantly engulfed by the bleaching lights of a news camera, his question kept rankling. "I wish I'd told him which of his policies I liked," I moaned. I could still see pieces of him amid the throng that now surrounded him. "Get back in there!" exclaimed my husband, propelling me Bloomberg-ward. And then, a miracle! A very tan hand came through the crowd. The mayor saw me approaching and hauled me in. "You asked me what policies of yours I liked," I said. "And I wanted to tell you." And I did (gun control, calories being posted, the trans fats work; Occupy Wall Street hadn't happened yet or I might have tempered my endorsement).

The moral of which is, I informed myself, that once you head off in the direction you want, unexpected allies often conspire to help you on your way. So why not head off with more lightheartedness? Why pine, I asked as I zipped up my suitcase.

And I was almost convinced.

For by now the rhythm of going away and coming back had started to seem so dazzlingly quick that when I returned to the city I was no longer disoriented. I picked up right where I'd left off, with just a slight amnesiac stutter in between, as if I were successfully living in more than one place at once, both Texas and New York, both the past and the present and almost the future, as if I were a Piaget child who'd learned the persistence of the beloved even when the beloved is out of sight. And yet—would loss always evoke a tormenting pang? Would that never fully change?

My next-to-last sublet was at the top of a brownstone in Clinton Hill. The owner of the apartment was a cinematographer, and everyone looked glamorous in his rooms. The light was diffuse, silky—no bulb, I soon discovered, was more than 40 watts. My first day I screwed in 100-watt bulbs so I could read, and the lamps remained beautiful but refused to part with their light: their shades were opaque chocolate brown, although their brass basses glowed like Aladdin lamps. One shone up at a little book tucked on a shelf: *Letters to a Young Artist*, modeled on the famous Rilke book but with missives from contemporary painters and sculptors. I read it on a chair the cinematographer had set beside the window.

"If you want to be a person who can survive on your art, you must clarify what can be exchanged with society before society will repay you," said the installation artist Xu Bing. "I was fearful and panicked . . . but I did it anyway," said Jessica Stockholder, a conceptual artist, talking about taking an important risk.

These were new thoughts, for me. I'd always assumed being panicked meant that you were doing the *wrong* thing, and that you ought to wait until you were calm before even contemplating making a change. So I'd actually relinquished the gift of my unhappiness; I'd squandered it, disowned it, telling myself, "Get calm. Don't even think about change until you're no longer upset. After all, you can't think clearly when you're so stirred up!"—and so I'd cast my life in emotional cement for year after year.

I'd remained in relationships too long and worked on projects too long, I saw now, gazing out the window at bustling Washington Avenue. Fear had always meant, to me, *Don't do it!*

And wasn't fear also an aspect of my clinging? After all, what did that pang mean when I left a place? It was mere attachment, in both the psychological and the spiritual sense. And it was the illusion that I would never have the good thing again. It was the illusion that something was wrong *because* I was sad, rather than that nothing was wrong *although* I was sad.

Of course the inevitability of loss is one of the big lessons of the Buddha. It is one of the essential truths, and as long as I tried to shield myself from it, I merely narrowed my life.

I'm writing this from a shockingly quiet apartment in Clinton Hill. Owned by an international journalist, its walls are covered with maps and its bookshelves must hold a hundred guidebooks. I think of it as the Invisible Apartment. It's perched on the roof of a brownstone, an apartment so tiny it can't be seen from the street, and it has no neighbors on any side except beneath its floorboards. When it's time to leave again I know I'll feel that pang, but I no longer fight it. It's even a kind of friend.

Life is all a sublet anyway, of course. We don't fully own even the bodies we live in; we can't stop them from changing. We cede them from year to year. And this knowledge of loss, I've discovered, is the salt that brings up the savor of all the rest—understanding that none of it is mine to keep. It's loss that provides the edge that makes the world sharply beautiful. Without it, life would pall somewhat; it would be far less intense. And the pang is the small price we pay.

I don't think I'll ever get to the level of real detachment—nor do I even seek it. Yet I've had these glimpses, as if I've taken a step back from my own life and can see the glittering pattern, all those scissor moments slicing us away from the past, letting us join the future, and I'm thankful for the perspective, which makes the inevitability of change easier to accept.

THE BUTTON KING:
THE DISCIPLINE OF THE NOTEBOOK

"A murderer was living around the corner, on Smith Street. I saw them filming *America's Most Wanted* in front of his building," said the old woman in the Key Food on Atlantic Avenue yesterday, talking to the manager in his booth. "You don't know who is a killer today and who isn't. Have a nice day." And off she shuffled. How could I not scribble down her words?

Joan Didion once claimed that she kept a notebook to remind herself of who she once was—the girl with the falling-down hem in a silk Peck & Peck dress. She proposed that her entries are "bits of the mind's string too short to use." In fact, her journal portrays rather completely a young glamour-besotted magpie hoping to build a safe nest out of snippets—hatcheck tickets and the tinsel from swizzle sticks, swatches of chinchilla stoles and recipes for oysters Rockefeller and orchid blossoms. Her journal, that is, captures who she was pretty comprehensively, via telling fragments.

There are other, more crucial, uses of the notebook. One has to do with those too-short bits of the mind's string. Halley's Comet, when I saw it in an Iowa field, was not bright enough to dim the moon, let alone illuminate the countryside in a wild blaze as it had in medieval times, when it terrified the populace. On the Bayeux

Tapestry it's a spike-geared wheel rolling across the heavens while a gathering of people point up, gaping at the omen, and King Harold, soon to be toppled by the invading William, cowers on his throne. When I saw it, it was the size of a thread of lint.

"There it is!"

"Where?" I asked.

"There! There!"

I followed the astronomer's jabbing finger to a smudge no bigger than a strawberry's beard bristle. That was my Halley's Comet. Still, I tweezed it out of the sky and set it in my book, its significance not to be revealed to me until many years later.

Similarly, the Button King, who Johnny Carson had on twenty-five years ago and who spent every night, all night long, gluing buttons to his car, to his pants and shirt, to the walls of his house—is still alive to me because he entered my book, and he, too, now seems like a camouflaged herald, a kind of annunciation angel spangled by a spotted strobe. Likewise the business card someone had dropped on Joralemon Street that revealed itself, on second glance, to be a mouse thinner than a dime, a rodent trod by so many oblivious feet that it had attained a certain city-buffed purity—exists for me today only because I placed the notation of its miraculously squashed form onto a page beside the thick-tongued middle-aged man three steps away shouting into the payphone to his mother: "It's unfair! Unfair!" As if his geriatric mother might at even this late hour make everything right.

In those days when I first returned to New York I was devoted to my notebook. And although it's been years since I cracked open that volume, I remember these things vibrantly. The act of writing inscribed them into me. There, the recorded figures purged themselves of the dross of the world; they acquired their own gravitas, emblems whose meaning took years to become clear—as if we must each gather our alphabet before we can speak; we must attract our materials before we can see what they promise. I would never have collected them if I hadn't simply happened to be keeping a notebook.

The vessel precedes significance. In a way, it *is* the significance: the commitment to register life. And beyond that—the conviction that perception itself salvages, saves. And beyond even that—the eerie experience of finally finding in myriad ragtag phenomena an underlying psychic connection, as if I've at last flipped over the fabric that made them appear separate and discovered long strands of embroidery thread linking one design with the next.

Three or four more crucial data points from those early days demand to be included: the elongated boots worn by the women in the elevator in the Condé Nast tower the first winter I worked for *Glamour*—the pointed snouts narrowing like blades, reminiscent of the footwear of Venetian courtiers—which I hauled into my journal along with the Incan-looking woman on the Borough Hall subway platform who plucked up her skirts, sank slightly, then—could it be? oh dear, yes—started to pee just before the 4 train arrived. The man who materialized just two stops later—Wall Street—clad in an expensively cut wool suit and gold cufflinks, as if sent specifically to illustrate some principle about Fortune's wheel. The man drowsing in a wheelchair on Forty-Third Street fifteen minutes later with a cardboard sign around his neck, *Insult me for $5.00* (apparently Fortune's wheel was bigger and swung lower than I'd imagined). The guy in a T-shirt printed with the words *Masturbation Isn't Illegal,* shoving a paper into my hand, which proved to be a leaflet protesting the use of scab workers by a construction company. All these moments of glinting significance exist for me only because I glued them down into my book.

Because, after all, what to do with life's fantastic drama? I was so excited to have arrived back in the city—having grown up in the Bronx but then lived in Iowa and Massachusetts—that now

I felt almost ill with joy. New York was a spectacle that demanded contemplation. Its simultaneity, its sheer wheels-within-wheels life made me feel privileged with a kind of sacred vision. "Thank you, thank you," some part of me was constantly saying. And because I didn't know what else to do with the extraordinary flickering scenes—because they filled me with a kind of burdening excitement—I transcribed them.

Besides, stupidity subsumes me unless I lodge my experience in words. Each dawn titrates into me a dollop of amnesia, of anesthesia, so that I become increasingly insensate. Instead of skin, I'm increasingly composed of Naugahyde. A friend of mine bought a book of gold leaf from an art supply store. Each page was the size of a Bazooka Joe comic. She was going to use it to gild a cake because in fact the stuff's edible. "Bring your finger close to it," she said, as I stared at the luminous surface shining like a chunk of halo. I pointed my finger ever closer. Suddenly the substance leapt, the gold coruscating and surging. My finger still trembled about an eighth of an inch away. "You don't actually paint with it. You sort of insinuate it onto the canvas," my friend explained. Many of us, when we were children, were composed of a substance just as sensitive. But we learned to ignore our responses. Without a countervailing force, we become more inanimate day by day.

So I write to make things real. Otherwise oblivion devours my days. One's whole life can pass in peripheral vision. We sense something is there but don't know how to turn. Or we turn and the thing turns just as fast. The notebook coaxes from the rim of consciousness some of the figures that lurk in the curtains, that linger behind the milk-glazed night sky which, in the city, admits no stars. A wall of light hides the ancient, blazing shapes. We below are as entrapped as the jumping beans in the shop next door to my Brooklyn apartment building—a heap of sealed-shut pods that tick night and day.

How does the manager put up with the clatter? Under the fluorescent light, the pods twitch. They flip like sleepers trying to get comfortable. They sound like a dozen people locked next door and tapping with their fingernails. Each pod is walnut brown and resembles a cherry pit; they're packed three to a Lucite cell. How does the storekeeper endure it, the banging of all those imprisoned spirits?

"I am a tiny caterpillar. I live inside a seedpod," says the orange paper laminated to the bin.

One day, to confront what it is that horrifies me, I buy a box of the beans. The manager reaches under the counter and produces a pamphlet. "I jump because I am eating a seed and spinning a cocoon," it says. "Hold me in your hand, give me a little sunshine, and I will jump like crazy."

Well, aren't we humans also like that, I ask myself, tapping out a song whose meaning we only occasionally understand? The heart thuds and ten years later, hearing the echo, we understand why. (Oh! I was *lonely!*) Our pulse flutters, and we shift, tracking someone with our eyes. In the night we wake to the radiator's clank as the heat comes on, and we hear our partner's breath, and a car siren suddenly rends the night—and for a moment we are confused as to what woke us. "I will turn into a tiny, harmless moth. Then I will bore a teeny hole in the pod and fly away."

Oh, so it's all about metamorphosis, I suddenly realize, as one of the beans throbs in my palm. One wasn't varnished shut after all! Out emerges the soul, the psyche, which means butterfly in Greek—emerges unless, of course, it doesn't because instead of transformation, as the pamphlet specifies, shouting the possibility: "THE CATERPILLAR HAS DRIED OUT, MOST LIKELY BECAUSE YOU HAVEN'T WATERED IT." Note to self: you have to water it. And to think, all this instruction in transfiguration was available for just two dollars and eight cents, tax included, right next door.

If only everything in the world came with a pamphlet, like the jumping beans. Since it doesn't, we with notebooks try to decipher the code, track the beats, the screech of the bus brakes, the clatter of a child's pencil racing over the fence-post bars. It's almost sufficient just to record what life is like this very instant—the powder-gold light clinging to the plane tree branches, the brittle leaves starting to curl. That momentary brush with a pencil makes the thing written about dawdle, stagger, allowing you to draw it into deeper focus. It sticks to you an instant and never really lets go.

Days with no writing are bad days. I become more obscure. I become the incomprehensible-feeling person I was when it seemed I wanted "too much" from my mother, who was harried and in a sort of despair, standing at the hall closet unable to swiftly sort out her four children's coats and hats and scarves (it all became a tangle)—and when I believed that my excessive, inalienable needs (I kept trying to slice them off like yellow rind off the bottom of one's foot, only to find they came back, pulsing) were horrifying, the clogged butt of a cat that follows you everywhere.

If only I could have been happy, I thought, back then! If only I could be one of those girls as gleaming as a plastic Barbie-doll case, and within which everything is neatly organized, the tiny dresses on their miniscule hangers, the even tinier shoes in their tiny drawer. Others' internal lives, I was sure, were like that. You could tell from their clean and pressed trousers, their hands folded calmly on their desks—whereas my cream-white tights instantly got grimy at the knee, my palms sweated, and the sky-blue Barbie case I in fact found on Mount Freedom Road in New Jersey commanded me to use it, in defiance of convention, to store a bounty of acorns. Because how astonishingly well crafted each acorn seemed, as if turned by a master of the lathe. Why abandon them to rot back into the earth?

Besides, I loved the important way the acorns rumbled as I carried them about—reminding me of my two big brothers' attaché cases, evidence of the valuable minds they possessed. Yet when autumn came around again and I sprang the locks—what a stink flew out! I stared, amazed by the pulpy, pungent mess inside. I scrubbed the case, but the thing was ruined. My mother agreed, and we threw it out. But how had the smear in me become the smear in it? Would everything I touched continue to reveal my secret?

In those childhood days I believed that the very least I could do for my mother was to be happy. It seemed an awful secret I carried that despite all my mother's gifts to me, my unhappiness remained. She so urgently wanted me to be content, and I couldn't manage it, and I felt sorry for my mother because of this, because of the acorns and clothing tangle. If only I could be happy, then it seemed that time itself would stagger, it would slow, bells of joy would toll their caramel circles, and the problem of life itself would be fixed. I assumed happiness was the cure to time.

But the golden currency of happiness was beyond me. Tears sprang to my eyes at the sight of a friend's baby brother in his playpen. There he stood silently in the winter living room whose gray spaces looked wrapped in gauze, in dust. Why bring children into the world, I wondered at the age of seven. Life was cold, with vast distances separating each of us. All this clumped up inside me—sadness, shame, need—a stuck-together heap, something untranslatable, craving expression but defying it. And I become that untranslatable girl again when I cease writing even a notebook. I am a neighbor to myself, tapping behind the wall, shifting, trying not to panic. Without the notebook, who knows what anything means?

I ask my writing students to keep journals. For the first two weeks I stipulate a page of observation a day. Think of your notebook less as a diary, I tell them, than as a verbal sketchbook. Capture as best you can the scenes you witness: the quality of light when you enter the bar or the church, the scent in the air, the exact color of that woman's dress.

"It's hard for me. I'm so in my head," sighs one student.

"That's why you should do it," I say. Because we are all so very much in our heads, sitting up there cross-legged and gazing out the eyeholes.

My antidote, keeping a notebook, is so potent that just knowing my students are doing it lets me see more—the limbs of the trees lit sea green and acid yellow in the October rain, which, I begin to notice, look pared, as if someone has scraped down their length with a blade.

"What's wrong with the trees?" my nephew's girlfriend asked. She was visiting Brooklyn from Milwaukee.

"Nothing. That's how they look. They're plane trees," I explained. She'd never seen such scabby branches, such camouflage-patterned trunks. If I write in my notebook I become my nephew's girlfriend, surprised by what's ordinary to me.

In goes *Insult me for $5.00* and boots like knives, and the glittering carnival of Fortune's wheel which once, for a brief while, flung me along in a yellow cab while I savored the midnight trip. In those days I wore a tight gray Lycra skirt drizzled with rhinestones and a sweater of thin black cashmere. The scent of cigarettes permeated. Snow funneled down out of the gauzy sky. I was happier than I'd ever been, and terrified of discovery, and at the same time I didn't believe that my secret life *could* be discovered because it was so fantastical and so at odds with my known, sane, cherished life that it verged on imaginary—a perfect secret.

But, as is the way with these things, it was mostly a secret from me; I discounted its significance. This is mere pleasure, I thought. Mere! The cab trundled down the FDR Drive at ten miles an hour on blacktop muffled thick with snow. The moon floated along behind the scrim of its atomized self. In that way it was reminiscent of the resinous substance that the evening and the city and I myself became when my foot swung over the threshold of the man I was involved with, and I was suddenly intoxicated and pulverized into a sort of Cray-pas dust in which everything interpenetrated—the distant ambulance sirens wailing, the scent of coffee drifting, the gauzy ambient glow in his apartment with all the electric bulbs dark, and my own skin twitching like gold leaf.

Halleluyah, I sang up to God. The awareness that I could have lived my whole life without this particular illumination ever washing through me made me both frightened and sharply grateful. Thank you, I muttered to my maker. When that time was over, though, I was relieved to return to sanity, to cease being terrified of discovery, and to find my apparently undestroyed, dear life waiting for me. In I crept. I did not want to live that other adventure any more. I was glad it was done, although it had left me altered.

All this goes into the notebook. I am the Button King, gluing buttons madly down on the pages, one mandala after the next, and the man shouting "it's unfair, it's unfair"—the way time wrenches everything away. I record the gingko tree opening its yellow fans. The reek of the Korean nail-polish place downstairs. The old woman at the Key Food talking about the local murderer. For of course there is always a murderer living around the corner. You don't know who is a killer today—the bus turning onto Livingston Street, the man with the knapsack—and yet here comes this old lady concluding: "Have a nice day." I smile. For an instant life tells me exactly what to do, and I hear it because I keep a notebook. A nice day—it's what my mother always wants for me. At ninety-one, she's keenly aware of how little time each of us has. How clear the message is today! Soon, however, the focus will shift, the message smudge, and I'll be back with the nonsensical ticks and beeps, and will have to begin writing again, to wrench some meaning from the machinery of life.

The notebook is a vessel for transformation. Jewish mystics used to believe that the world presents innumerable smashed pieces of vessels with divine light clinging to them. It is each individual's responsibility to rescue the captive sparks. Notebook-keepers have their own particular method of collecting the shards, trying to uncage the shimmer.

And we assume, as well—a central tenet of the notebook tribe—that what's locked in silence begins to turn, to fizz and rot. I hoarded that wealth of rumbling acorns because I craved the riches that my brothers possessed. Their minds, their being, were important to my parents because they were boys. The attaché case with its jabbing angles, the locks that shot open with pistol bangs, the graph-paper notebooks stacked inside—all spoke of my parents' esteem. How I hoped my female ooze could be transfigured somehow by imitating the cerebral piousness of my brothers, their toting of important objects through the streets of the Bronx.

And yet, despite the reassuring rattle of those acorns, what madness to tote one's feral cargo from one year to the next! In my own case, the hidden aspect was the female side of me, which I had estranged as unimportant, demeaning, mad, a leaky, degrading although apparently inalienable part. Then, for a brief while out she sprang. She owned the city. And after, I retained a certain strength, the conviction of a kind of beauty where before I'd been ashamed.

Still, of course, awareness of one's nature isn't easy. There's always another aspect to admit. Dare we open up? We hear the soft tick, then the loud knock. "It's a murderer!" our soul cries. "Don't unlock the door!" And our soul is right: the neighbor, the hidden self, is here to carry us from the old life to the new. We thought we knew what love was, what lust was, what children were, what parents were, but now we see more, gazing through the eyes of our neighbor, the murderer of our old way in the world.

The discipline of the notebook teaches attention to life, which itself is a doorway. What your own eye is drawn to, the emblems that haunt your pages, the dreams that won't let you forget them, the gold that your finger attracts—no need to know in advance what these omens signify. There are no bits of the mind's string too small to carry meaning. Unknown neighbors step near, tapping on paper walls, trying to show you unexpected passageways out of the sealed-shut vessel of the self.

Looking back I see a dozen harbingers of change. They were all apparently disappointing and even ugly aspects of the world made lovely—made holy—simply by being looked at, by being chosen, by being marveled over. For an endless instant their meaning is clear. Halleluyah, my soul cries out at a gleam from a rushing comet, at the rhinestones' flash, at the whole wheel of life, glimmering, spinning, rolling one incarnation into the next.

A Summons to Riverdale

My exterminator couldn't talk to me because he was at the U.S. Open. That's when I knew that the bedbug crisis in New York had really gotten out of hand. What fortunes were being made! He'd taken my call only because I'd interviewed him once for *The New York Times*. Now, when I started asking about the particulars of treating my ninety-one-year-old parents' apartment, he said: "Can you please call me during normal business hours?" In the background I could hear genteel applause. Then silence. Then applause again.

"Okay," I said. "Thank you. Enjoy the game!" I was anxious not to annoy him.

I was in the airport in Atlanta, between flights. My parents had had the inspection dog in on Monday, and he'd indicated, with a lift of his paw, that my mother's bed was infested, as was the living room couch. My gut plunged with dismay when my father told me the news because I recalled the mayhem that bedbugs had caused in my life six years earlier, but my father was surprisingly philosophic. "No need to come home, Bon," he opined calmly, and then my mother seized the phone: "STAY IN TEXAS! WE ARE PERFECTLY FINE! IT'S THE START OF THE SEMESTER, TAKE CARE OF YOUR CLASSES."

"What are you talking about?" I yelled back almost as loudly, as if on ship-to-shore radio. "You have no idea! Of course I'm going to come back."

"DON'T! AT OUR STAGE OF THE GAME, IT'S NOT A BIG DEAL. WE'RE JUST GOING TO LIVE WITH IT!"

She was perfectly sincere, sad to say.

"I'm coming!" I said, and I went.

"Don't bring anything! Not a thing!" I'd told my parents.

My plan was to take them up to the Tarrytown Marriott while their apartment was prepared and treated. My husband, who travels constantly for business, would use some of his thousands of points on hosting them. The night before my flight to New York, I trolled the local Walmart in order to outfit my parents. Boxer shorts, check. Stretch slacks for my mother, check. I called to ask my father his pants size, and he yelled: "*What* are you doing?"

"I'm in Walmart. Buying fresh clothing for you to wear so you don't bring the bugs with you. Just tell me your pants size."

It was as if I were calling from the moon. He couldn't make head or tail of it. "Say that again?" he said, and I did. But then, after a moment's silence in which I registered his absolute bewilderment, he told me his waist and leg measurement.

"Is this Bedbug Bonnie?" asked my brother Ken when I answered the phone in the Walmart parking lot. It was actually my first ever foray to Walmart, and I could understand how America was so besotted with it. $200 for four days' clothing for three people, including a suitcase! But my brother's teasing surprised me in the midst of feeling competent, and recalled to me my old family role as youngest and goofiest child. And I was almost grateful to him, for his words were like a bulletin finally revealing why I'd had difficulty taking myself seriously in life. "*I'm* not the one with bedbugs. Your parents are," I observed loudly, for once not letting his little joke pass unchallenged.

"You're right," said my brother Ken.

I paused, blinking, with my hand on the upraised trunk lid of the car.

"Thanks for going, Bon," he added in a different, somber tone of voice, and I felt, in a bittersweet way, like a grown-up.

But now here came my parents out the door of their Bronx apartment building. And what did my father have at his side? A little pink fabric valise! "I told you not to bring anything!" I exclaimed.

My father shrugged. "She insisted," he said simply. I was touched because I knew that my father realized my mother was taking a dangerous and ill-informed risk by bringing that suitcase.

"Well, she can't bring it. It's impossible." I extracted from my own suitcase a big black garbage bag I'd brought for just this kind of occurrence. I deposited the valise into the plastic bag, twisted the bag shut and set it in the trunk of my father's car. Then I ushered in my parents: my father a gentle, modest white-haired man in pressed trousers, and my mother a shrunken but eager woman bent over a metal walker. How delicate they seemed, and I felt a moment's worry for them, that they'd placed themselves in my hands.

My mother settled herself into the back of the emerald Camry, wearing her big dark plastic Yoko Ono wraparound glasses, useful against cataracts. My father sat beside me, and the whole drive up to Tarrytown my father anticipated and second-guessed the GPS, which I'd brought from Texas. "Does she ever make a mistake?" asked my father.

"Never," I lied, recalling rare instances when she'd lead me in a circle, chanting over and over, "When possible, make a legal U-turn."

"Get over a lane, Bon. It's going to be a sharp left!"

"Stop, Dad! Don't talk!" I barked. "You're getting me edgy. I only want to take directions from her." Immediately, of course, I regretted my harshness, and privately vowed to be respectful.

"Left-hand exit in .5 miles," intoned the GPS. But my father said nothing for the rest of the trip, and I felt sorry because I knew he was upbraiding himself, and all around us out the windows the beautiful Saw Mill River Parkway swept by. How lush these trees were, after the parched, rangy trees of Texas with their alligator-coruscated trunks, their splayed branches clawing for rain, their leaves of pigskin mauve. In truth there was a way that my life in Texas had always seemed the very height of unlikely to me. I was going on four years there, having landed a tenure-track job, and yet felt the entire time that someone might pinch me and I'd wake up in my New York bed. "What a strange dream!" I'd exclaim, although whether it was Texas or adulthood itself that was fantastic I couldn't say. Now I was back in deciduous, familiar terrain, the green shimmering.

"This really is a park way," I thought, having never quite set observant eyes on it before, and I relaxed, happy to be with my parents, who, while worried about their situation, were obviously happy to be with me.

My parents loved the concierge lounge. While I was on the phone with various extermination companies, my parents sampled the amenities—the pasta salad, the hunks of cheese and sesame crackers, the pristine monolithic rotunda of Oreo cheesecake, and the glass of white wine I divided into three portions and encouraged them to drink. Normally my mother restricts herself to the sardine plate at the Blue Bay Diner on Johnson Avenue. "Hold the potato salad, and please give me extra lettuce," is her usual request. But now, transported out of their usual environment, which they hadn't ventured from in years since they like to be near their doctors, and with a free banquet spread before them, they decided to experiment.

"This cheesecake tastes very fresh!" said my father, licking his fork. "And what an unusual flavor!" Jeopardy blared, and businessmen all around my parents shouted out answers, and my mother shouted out answers too. At the commercial break she turned to the convivial men at the next table. "That's my daughter. She's visiting from Texas, where she's a professor at a university."

I turned my back and hunched lower over the phone in a corner, discussing options with the various bedbug kings who have recently flourished. Which approach to take? And how to get all the work done in just three days? I'd long ago accepted an invitation to dine that Saturday in the home of my department chairman. After three years at the university, I'd been asked. On the one hand it seemed absurd not to cancel—my parents were of transcendent importance! On the other, I believed it would communicate to my department chair (especially coming right after my semester on leave) that I wasn't really committed to my Texas life and job, besides annoying him by creating a problem with his dinner party. And if I lost this job it seemed as if my own adult independence—that will-o'-the-wisp—would be lost as well. Still, I recalled to myself those absurd characters in Russian literature who fly into conniption fits over an ambiguous glance from a bureaucratic superior. What to do? What to do? But—there was no need to decide yet! Perhaps my parents really could be rid of the bugs in three days—after all, several companies promised this.

Still, to properly prepare an apartment to be treated for bedbugs is a colossal task. Each drawer must be opened and its contents laundered and sealed, each closet and bureau shelf must be emptied. It's good to throw away what you can. I'd hoped that in the years since I'd had bedbugs myself all this would have changed—but no.

And meanwhile, the back of my mind carried the uncomfortable advice of a friend whose parents had recently passed away: "Clear out as much as you can each visit, so it isn't so overwhelming at the end."

My parents still live in the three-bedroom apartment in Riverdale in which they raised four children. They own innumerable things. They have the kind of TV that's lodged in a mahogany case. Atop this TV sits a bronze statuette of Ben Franklin in wire-rim spectacles emanating a message of humane civility, a sort of domestic tutelary genius. In my brothers' old bedroom, now my father's study, a real stuffed hawk with spread wings and gleaming glass eyes surveys tiers of curios. How could all the necessary objects possibly get vacuumed and dry-cleaned and set in bags? And yet—services now existed!

I spoke to one woman who employed out-of-work actors. And another whose team of men would ride the subway up to the Bronx with their own PackTite heating machine. All my parents' furniture could be spirited out of their home to be fumigated off-premises while their apartment was steamed. It was possible to invest one's entire inheritance in ridding an apartment of bedbugs. And why not? If only one could be guaranteed they wouldn't return!

"You must think I'm very fat," my mother said in the elevator down from the lounge. Indeed the Walmart shirt and slacks I'd bought her flowed around her. "I'm a size six. The same as you! But you think I'm some kind of fatso!"

My father said: "I don't think I can go on this way."

"What do you mean, Dad?" I asked, feeling suddenly ill. Did he think he needed to move back to his apartment although it wasn't treated? Was he feeling too depressed by the upheaval?

"I need to have a belt."

He wrung my heart! His hands were dug into his pockets and hoisted upwards, holding his cuffs aloft, as in fact they'd been all evening, and he hadn't once complained. "Oh, Dad!" I exclaimed. "Of course you can have a belt! I'm so sorry. We'll get one tomorrow." Although, with all I needed to do, I couldn't imagine how or where.

My mother said: "When can I have my valise?"

"What do you want from it?"

"The valise!"

"Well, you can't have it. I told you not to bring it, and you did. You seem to think I'm making up these rules. I'm not! This is just what's necessary! You have to take absurd-seeming measures to defeat these bugs, and you're not allowed to diverge from them one iota."

My mother gazed at me. "When can I have my shoes?" she said.

She was wearing big brown bedroom slippers I'd bought for my father since her own Walmart shoes, she insisted, didn't fit. Her real shoes were encased in a plastic bag in the closet.

But how could she be carrying on like this? My head pounded. "I'm going to throw them out the window, Mom, if you don't stop!" I screeched, on the verge of tears.

I opened the door to the hotel room and let them in, then went off to buy some safety pins for my father's pants. When I returned my parents were chastened, loving, grateful, in a way that made me sad.

That evening my father and I watched a baseball game in the lounge while my mother rested. He explained to me the way the game was played. I'd thought I'd known since childhood how the game was played, but actually there were many crucial aspects of which I'd been oblivious. My father told me about the batter's strike zone, and how the opposing pitcher was very well acquainted with what kind of pitches each particular batter would be tempted to hit. He mentioned that, growing up in Brooklyn, there had been lots of wonderful uncut fields nearby in which he enjoyed playing baseball. "What was your favorite position?" I asked, picturing him on first or else poised on the pitcher's mound—dramatic roles anyone would want.

"Infield," he said. I nodded. It was the maverick, ranging-around position that takes care of all the others, it seemed to me—although actually I hadn't known he enjoyed playing any sport. I'd known him only as a worried and often burdened-seeming man, although he loved tossing a softball around with my brothers in Saxon Woods Park. But when I was a girl the slam of the ball into the glove, the admittedly beautiful arc of the flung ball through the air, had seemed frivolous to me—something mechanical, inane. I'd read novels in a lawn chair. Now it seemed a language, a message from a father to his child, steady, bone-deep, and reassuring. You can do it. This is how. I'm here. You'll be okay. And, watching the ball game with my father, I somehow received some of that guidance.

My parents' apartment, when I swung open the door the next morning, seemed exactly as elegant and neat as ever—it had a hushed, waiting quality, and was, as usual, as composed as a museum. What had I expected? Giant bugs playing music and trying on my parents' clothes, as in a Kliban cartoon? Well, pandemonium is what I expected, and it's what I went about imposing.

My parents' cleaning woman and I dragged forth from the closets all their secret and long-exiled contents—the horn-shaped leather purse my sister Anita had worn bandolier-style in high school, a tortoiseshell-enamel radio big as an ice chest, and several sea-green bottles full of buttons, each one as distinct as a treasured personality: the rounded chocolate-velvet buttons, the intricate faux carved-ivory ones, and the nautical brass buttons that seemed to swell with pride. These buttons had been my very first play things; I preferred them to dolls, whose characters seemed both drastically limited and frightening. But now, in a fit of desperate haste, I threw all this away.

I'm helping my parents, I'm helping my parents, I consoled myself as I worked, for each time I disposed of an object it actually seemed an act of infidelity—as if I were expunging memory itself. Goodbye to the yellowed lace tablecloth that restored to me, at a glance, a Passover when my sister was in full voice and my father's brother clapped always an instant too late, a clumsy and dear man; the cloth might have been bleached white again if I wasn't in such a hurry. Goodbye to the skeins and skeins of beautiful Icelandic yarn stuffed in the bureau—not Anita's, since she'd carried hers to her own apartment when she moved out after college. My mother hadn't knit in three decades. I could hardly remember her ever knitting but apparently it had once been an obsessive passion, as there were entire quivers of needles and a wall of fabulous yarn as strong and clean as if it had just been spun from freshly shorn polar sheep. The more I snatched out, the more popped into view, as though, if only I could take time to really examine the contents of this bureau, I would discover a woman quite different from the mother I'd youthfully misperceived.

But time was what I lacked. Out went boxes of blue linen stationery, packs of fading empty Jewish New Year's cards, decorative placemats from various decades of family meals. I was astonished to encounter, in one of my mother's desk drawers, in a bulging manila envelope, the object of my first passion: a stuffed koala, eyes askew, paws fallen off, regarding me from across the years. Who knew that my mother loved me so much she had saved this? And yet wasn't this mere clutter? The bear's open head, with the stuffing effusing out, surely provided a good harborage for bugs.

I tossed it, with a sense that I was defiling our past. In fact, my entire effort of clearing—throwing out the couch, finding in my father's drawer a gold bracelet from my mother's mother that dated back to 1903 and which I set into a big clear plastic bag to be saved, finding, as well, a whole tooth down to the root, a feral molar almost as long as my pinkie (whose was it? Why had it been saved? I'll never know, but I tossed it), and discovering as well in the very back of a drawer secret psychological notes my father had made having to do with shyness (oh, I'd never known that that was the malady he believed he suffered from! To think that it had a *name*!) And then I read: "When your soul knows a certain action is the correct thing to do, then summon the nerve and do it once and for all, although the decision temporarily brings disorder," written out in my father's neat, elegant handwriting, and I hunched, socked in the gut. There was a change in my own life that I'd put off and put off, and yet wasn't it true that something in me knew, had known for years, what action was correct? Why, it was the "disorder" that had kept me paralyzed because I hadn't realized, until that instant, that the disorder would be temporary! Nor had I believed in the soul, with its archaic majesty, its unfakeable clarity, until I saw the word etched in my father's hand.

There was more to read, many neatly written out pages. I flung them into a bag, telling myself, I'll read this in the future; they are at the very core of understanding my father and also of understanding myself. Yet I knew I would almost certainly never find those pages again—and meanwhile during all of this, my entire effort of cleaning, all this frantic disgorging and sorting, I felt I was committing an act of almost incomprehensible violence against my delicate parents, who take so much better care of things than I do.

I'm careless with objects, living mostly in my head. My parents are intellectual but also value the physical, real world. They have a wood-handled Botanical Gardens umbrella of the Enid Haupt glass pavilion that they've kept for over twelve years; I've been able to hold onto almost nothing that long. And here—hauled out of a dark far corner of the hall closet—my hands clasped a green velvet umbrella I'd given my mother fifteen years ago. I'd thought she'd thrown it out! I'd bought the thing hastily, in a shop I passed on my way to my mother's birthday celebration. From her expression when I handed her the velvet umbrella I knew she found it ugly and would never use it, and indeed she never had. At the birthday restaurant, she'd set it aside in a crabbed, dismissive way, and I felt again what I often had as a child—my insufficiency. But here it was, not abandoned, not given up on, stalwartly held onto in the back of her coat closet! Ah, she kept better faith with me than I ever did with her, I thought. It pierced my heart, and then I threw it away.

Now it seemed to me that what was worst in me had been let loose upon my parents. I wept as I cleaned. I was their impatient, impractical daughter, the one who had lost one of my father's rabbit-fur-lined gloves the single day I borrowed them in college, and who let slip from my thoughtlessly overloaded arms after my bas mitzvah a silver candleholder, into which was bashed forever the nubbly texture of the pavement of 239th Street. Valuables should not be entrusted to me, I'd long understood. Nor had I wanted them. And now the most valuable thing in my life, my parents, were in my care. I sensed that in my bug-phobic hurry I was disposing of a hundred magic items. Away with the no-longer-worn pearl clip-on earrings as big as cameos. Away with the real leopard-fur shoes warped into Aladdin's lamps. It was as if I were still the clumsy, obtuse child I'd been in elementary school, unable to understand the significance of what was around me but suddenly endowed with adult power.

For my parents inhabit the world with far greater awareness than I, as if they think and feel in a language that has five words for each of my one. They sigh and flinch at nuances indiscernible to me. And they have a sense of life's reality that I completely lack. I live as if I'm make-believe, and nothing actually counts. I'll get another childhood, another first romance, another long marriage, and, although I'm entering menopause, I'll still bear children. Everything in my life allows for a do-over, I seem to believe. While, in contrast, my parents believe through and through that this is their only go 'round. Yes, something might endure after death, but they won't get all this again. Their lives have a palpability to them, whereas my own is so suffused with denial that it seems I'm tipped back in the dentist's chair, floating on anesthetic gas, able to dream an entirely different life for myself should I care to, but I simply don't care to, just yet.

My mother is living now, and has her whole life long. She's worked from the age of fourteen through eighty-five. My parents came of age during the Depression. They sprang from circumstances I could never really comprehend—barely scraping-by Yiddish homes. My mother spoke often of her childhood poverty. Their possessions had a significance to them that even now I couldn't fully grasp. As long as the objects existed there was a chance that one day I might grow into a fuller understanding. But now, desperate to purge the bugs, haste dominated.

The more I threw away, the easier it was to keep throwing. A certain desperation—allowed to persist since my earliest youth and compelling as a revealed truth, as if the reality is that one ought to be in a panic, perhaps a remnant of pogrom days—reigned supreme, and I no longer knew if what I was doing, all this heaving into the garbage, was good or bad, warranted or gratuitous. I opened a bottom drawer and my glance fell on a two-inch-thick wad of bills, what turned out to be seven hundred dollars in twenties. Horror gripped me—what if this were one of the drawers I'd asked a service to clear out? I stuffed the bills into my wallet to give my father that evening, recalling that he had always had a cache of money with which to tip workmen and in case of emergencies—whereas

I, shamefaced, was often unable to tip when deserved, and roamed my city with an empty wallet, like a child.

I was recklessly dismantling my parents' kingdom. It ought to be my brothers—both older, highly responsible—caring for my parents: one is a doctor and the other is an engineer, but both were busy with their lives, and my parents' care was entrusted to me. Which would have been laughable if it weren't frightening, for I felt myself to be the same rabid, overheated girl I used to be when I was in high school and came home from a date near midnight, and then stayed awake pillaging the kitchen, eating everything my hands fell on in a bacchanalia of appetite. Only when I stopped eating would disgust at my behavior crash down and subsume me, and so I kept devouring. And then, from behind the wall, came the voices of my parents. They were in bed, discussing their children. They mentioned my name with love. My jaw froze, and their voices came louder.

They were worried about me. Would I get into a good college? Was I staying out too late with my boyfriend? My heart crumpled— I somehow hadn't thought they thought about me when I was not physically before them! Don't worry about me, Mom and Dad, I wanted to shout. I'm not worth it! Take care of yourselves! My gaze fell on the stub of challah that was left, the stump of remaining cheese. Why, I could devour my parents down to the very bones. What a raging hunger possessed me! I remained stock-still although I knew I was transgressing, listening, listening, until I no longer heard the voices. If only my parents could be protected from me!

Later I recalled how Frederick and Steven Barthelme had gambled away their parents' entire legacy. Their parents had been frugal; they had worked hard; they knew the value of a dollar. And after they died their novelist/professor sons inherited a surprising amount—over a quarter of a million dollars—which they quickly gamed away on the riverboats moored off the coast of Mississippi, both brothers suddenly addicted gamblers. What we can't bear to have, we throw away.

"Thank you so much," my mother said, that evening, in the concierge lounge. "You're working so hard!"

I shook my head and looked away. "Not really, Ma," I said.

I bought a glass of white wine and split it in two, and my mother, who usually drinks only on Passover, smiled and said: "It's such a nice sensation! It gives you the feeling your problems are floating away. You can't worry about anything!"

I nodded yes.

But soon she was sleepy, and drowsed on her bed.

"I'm sorry that I gave you that wine that made you sleepy," I said.

"No," she said, smiling with her eyes closed. "I'm still enjoying it. It's a good feeling."

She awoke a few hours later and we stayed up talking, she lying beside my father, who slept on his back. How long had it been since we had open-ended time before us, just she and I?—years, certainly. She told me certain things I'd never known. That she hadn't liked to go home to her mother after a work day. That her mother had treated her like a drudge. That she hadn't even loved her mother, eventually. This I didn't believe. I recalled the tenderness with which she used to speak to her elderly parent, and the little photo of her mother she kept on her bureau and which was currently sealed in a plastic bug-proof bag, and it occurred to me that her feelings towards her mother had changed now that she herself faced death, a circumstance from which even her mother couldn't save her.

Or was I wrong? For on this night my mother seemed urgently to want to communicate her secrets. "By the time I had four children, I no longer liked her at all," she said of her mother. "I never really found great affection for her."

"It's so sad!" I said.

"Yes. She didn't take good care of me."

There was a long silence. Her eyes were shut. My father was asleep beside her.

"Do you want to go to sleep?" I asked.

"I don't know. I'm enjoying talking to you," she said.

"There's no enough," I said after a while, into the long silence. "It's like looking at the sea. Or into a fire. One is never done. That's how I feel, being with you. I'm always enjoying. I never want it to end. There's no enough."

But she didn't answer. She was asleep.

The apartment was treated the next day. Two men arrived in a snub-nosed little white van and sprayed my parents' apartment with freezing carbon-dioxide gas—a contact kill—stepping from room to room with a nozzled hissing machine like the device in *Ghostbusters*. The entire time they worked, I was happy. Now we were getting somewhere!

Still, the house was stripped, the elaborate blue-and-green draperies that had decorated the rear wall of the living room—the pride of the apartment—had been yanked off and the blank scuffed white paint exposed along with surprising, glaring bandages of plaster; all the walls, once so densely decorated, were bare, the couch was missing, discarded, and the remaining spindly looking wood furniture huddled in the middle of the floor while these men with their outer-space machine worked. What did it all mean, I wondered, pacing after them as if contemplating a nightmare and not a necessity, why had I been so frantic to reduce my parents' home to this? After all, "reality is distracting you," a therapist had once told me, meaning that it was possible for such a perfect fit to exist between actual conditions and your psychic needs that you could seamlessly curtain away your own neurosis.

I could not possibly save my parents from what really threatened—their increasingly aged state always came as a shock—and so why not allow obliterating desperation to consume me? My parents were like the porcelain man and woman my sister Anita had once let me borrow for Show and Tell, and which I blithely stowed in my dress pocket. What a nice little reassuring clack they made as I strode along! Later that morning in class I reached into my pocket, and held aloft before my staring classmates twin decapitated figurines shattered at the throat. I blushed, pulsing.

The smiling round faces had remained in my pocket! Oh, how stupid I'd been! But of course I shouldn't have trusted myself with the fragile figures. Contact with me harmed things, I'd long understood. My depressed mother had felt my touch as sticky, clingy, excessive, when I was a child hauling her back to an undesired reality. She'd been unable to attend to me, and it had cast a particular enchantment over me, had steeped me in the illusion that I was forever trying to accomplish magic tricks, like a child trying to tie her shoes by simply weaving her fingers about over the ladders of holes. My mother's only half-seeing gaze converted me into someone unreal, whose foot couldn't leave an imprint, and who therefore hastened slipshod, desperately, through her work because she could never get it right, could never really achieve, so why not rush? My parents created a half-finished person and entrusted themselves to her care.

And to her the ripped-down curtains, the bare walls, the whole aspect of a madhouse seemed natural. Apt. As if, if I could finally display the full scope of my incapacity, my parents would just have to become the vigorous parents they once were, long ago, in a time before even I could remember. But they did not.

When the men finished, four hours later, I signed papers and thanked them, and got into the car to drive to a Bed, Bath, and Beyond in Yonkers for mattress encasements. After these were put on, the entire apartment needed to be treated with pesticide.

The GPS froze on the way to Yonkers, and I got lost, and tried to intuit how to go (how difficult could it be to find "Central Park Avenue"?). At last I despaired and turned around to go to the hotel, and ended up calling my father. "I don't really know the way," he said. "Yes, you do," I answered. He had the Bronx and Westchester County in his bones. And sure enough he directed me back without a mistake, his voice coming over the cell phone. I wept silently, thankful for his impeccable guidance, his voice in my ear now that everything was in a state of dissolution, with so much consigned to oblivion. His voice in my ear was ineffably moving, I realized, because I did not believe I deserved it, and I suddenly understood in a flash, peering into the night, the town names he predicted shimmering in the distance at long last—that I would never believe I deserved it. This was adulthood, after all. Time, at last, to accept such things.

Still, how impossibly sweet it was to receive what I'd craved my whole life long, this fatherly attention and reassurance. Ah, my stupid brothers, to forgo this! My father said little between the far-apart exits, he was an old, old tired man but he was still on the line, the receiver to his ear as I drove on. A clamor rang out from the room behind him, chairs scraping, shouts goodbye, but still my father remained, and it suddenly seemed to me, with a pang of sharp wild green painful hope such as I'd never felt before (no, *this* was adulthood!—hope), that perhaps there was a possibility, after all, of being transformed by what he was giving me, maybe it wasn't too late for me, not too late after all—my father hadn't given up! He wanted me to make it, he wanted this for me, to become a full, complete person at last, a person who could quit making mistakes, who no longer needed to screw up, who could occupy her life, and who could survive without him when she had to, a person worthy of attention despite the fact that I felt almost like a thief to take it from my father now, but take it I did, pitying him all the while, for I could hear how, at ninety-one, exhausted he was, with the whole long day behind us.

I arrived back almost two hours late, despite his expert directions. I ran up to the concierge lounge, and there they were, my father behind the glass, slightly hunched, haggard, standing up and peering out toward the elevator, the last two guests in the see-through room. "Bon, you're here at last!" my father exclaimed. And he clasped my hand. "Thank God!" he said.

"We're staying on at the Marriott," my mother declared. "Another week, at least. Until after the second treatment is done. It's very nice here."

"I'll say it is!" I agreed. "But won't you miss Riverdale?"

"I lived in Riverdale forty years. It's good to get a change," she said.

"What do you like about it?"

"The people are lovely, the food is good, everything is taken care of for you. I'm having a vacation here!"

Early the next morning a limousine picked me up to take me to LaGuardia. There was no shuttle or bus service from the Tarrytown Marriott. The driver wore a beautiful wool suit. There were peppermints and bottles of water beside me. I felt mortified by the sloppy oversized Walmart gray drawstring sweatpants I was wearing, and my pocketbook, encased in a black plastic bag.

At the department chair's dinner party that night I drank red wine. The senior poet in the department sat across from me, beside a fiction writer from Bulgaria. The only others present were the department chair and his wife and my husband. It was a tiny gathering, and I felt happy to be there. My house was just three houses down from the department chairman's, and it had tickled me to set off for the party at almost the instant I wanted to arrive. I'd walked half a block to arrive at the festivities while also having traveled half the continent to reach them.

And yet even as I savored the evening, the Bronx called to me. My life in Texas seemed paper thin compared to what was going on back there.

So much remained to be done. Next time I would be calmer. I would take my time. I would decisively turn the corner on eliminating the bugs. I felt confident of success, and couldn't wait to dive back in. After that I would be able to really immerse in my life here, and perhaps then too my life among the Osage orange trees with their bejeweled DayGlo fruit and the post oaks with their sprawling umbrella-prong branches, as well as the department meetings, the pressures to publish—my life as a tenure-track college professor, that is—would no longer seem so unlikely.

But first the living room carpet needed to be steam treated, the drapes in my brother's room to be bagged and dry-cleaned, and perhaps there was a pesticide application to be overseen. I couldn't wait. For I'd found it marvelously satisfying to help my parents, and I'd keenly loved the time we'd spent together, thrust from our homes and our usual routines. I smiled at the department chair across the table. I would fly back and drive my parents home in a week. This entire episode, odd as it was, was a strange, awful gift, the gift of a lifetime. Who knew when it would end?

AFTERWORD:
MESSAGE FROM THE SHADES

"You de-realize things," said the man with whom I'd been involved. "You don't allow the pain of your situation to seem real."

I was sitting at the time in my living room, hunched forward on the couch, shoving the phone to my ear. I pushed so hard that a fiery circle blazed the side of my head, while my eyes were clasped shut so I would not lose a syllable. "Tell your husband about us," he said. "Especially if you're going to stay. You can't found intimacy on a lie."

"Really?" I asked, the very last—and perhaps most laughable—statement of my innocence.

And yet I'd heard a radio psychologist advocate not burdening one's partner with information that didn't really pertain to him or her. Did my information really pertain? I was at the very end of the phase where I put my revelations into notebooks rather than acting on them. I was, however, already acting on the revelation that I must give up this man. This was, in fact, our last conversation.

We said goodbye—he with sad bitterness, but also kindness, and I with relief. Among other things, I'd missed being able to think, during the time that I saw him. I missed the calm functioning of my mind. Now I set the phone back into its hook, and went straightaway to my desk and turned on my computer. But the words lingered around me in a kind of mist: "You de-realize things." That's what it is, I told myself, suddenly sitting up, crossing my arms as if from a chill. That is my main problem.

De-realize: make unreal, and also, nullify one's realization. Put it to sleep. Inhale deeply in the field of poppies and loosen one's grasp on the truth you've won, allowing it to fall back into unconsciousness.

Do women de-realize more than men? It certainly seems likely. Our culture physically de-realizes us, of course, air-brushing our photos far more frequently than those of men. And women are still the minority perspective: our movies are almost all directed and written by men, and the books discussed in the book reviews are famously disproportionately by men, as well. In the classes I now teach at the University of North Texas, men volunteer to speak far more than women do. Many women continue to assume that our perspective is aberrant, anomalous, distorted, excessive in some way. And, personally, I myself had preferred the peace of de-realization. I was terrified of change.

So for one last summer I continued in my dream state. It was spring when that man and I said goodbye, and all summer I wrote, and then swam on the weekends with my husband at a beautiful pond in Connecticut, and during the week I composed sentences while the air conditioner in my office thrummed. But an odd melancholy gradually set in. One day followed another and I felt I was drifting. I was waiting and I had no idea for what. I couldn't picture what would shatter my thrall. During the affair I told myself I couldn't tell what was true about my marriage since the affair distorted things. After, I told myself that I wouldn't be able to discern the truth until my life grew still and I had forgotten that man. I swam in the yellow-green pond between two rafts, in one direction doing the crawl, my face immersed, in the other direction doing the backstroke, face tipped toward the sun, lids shut, orange-pink blazing behind my eyes.

What is the beauty from the underworld that the woman in the archetypal story must obtain?

In *The Wizard of Oz*, it is the dream space, the Kodacolor land that Dorothy inhabits once she falls, and in which she can experience the furies and oppositions that Kansas life forbids. Underworld beauty is the gold sun ball that the frog brings up in his mouth; it is the box of Chanel No. 5, all exclusively pristine ivory trimmed with black, which the pupil offers the teacher in *An Education*—and which the teacher refuses because she knows its cost: the pupil abandoned school for a tryst in Paris. It is Cher in *Moonstruck*, dressed to the nines, at the opera with her passionate taboo brother-in-law-to-be with the gnarled hand. It is what you aren't supposed to love, but do, despite yourself. In my own case, beauty from the underworld was also apparent ugliness. It was the messy, dirty, forbidden, dissociated, buried, feral places where my truth got hidden and which the official education didn't recognize.

I myself revered the official version of reality, my childhood *New York Times* with its gaunt, grim columns of type, its imposing Gothic scimitar blades and steely pennants. Still, so much of what is important was not acknowledged by this 1960s official version, and I didn't acknowledge it either. I wanted to leave behind what I had inside me—the endless internal mess. Chekhov reported that it took years for him to give up the slave mentality. His grandfather had been a serf, and his father had purchased his own freedom. But it took the writer himself many years to "squeeze the slave out of [him]self, drop by drop." I too had had a long transition. And ultimately it was underworld beauty that freed me.

Images that won't depart!—that return for you time and again, in dreams, in movies, in street scenes you note out of the corner of your eyes, in wishes that hollow you if you don't pursue them—all these came for me. Shades from the deep that haunted, that stationed themselves in the periphery of awareness, that wanted me, it seemed, to have a real life, a full life, and not the self-mesmerization to which I consigned myself. Underworld vision! It is, I found, one's own secret, alive, pulsing, vibrant, native view of things when you allow yourself to make the connections, the rational and the irrational ones, the ones that stem from the seat of your "lower" passions as well as your "upper" ones. How I had denied the body and its messages—as if it were merely a container for me. As if what it meant by love and what I meant by love were two very different things.

"When you don't know what to write, write the Cinderella story," quoted the man with whom I'd been involved. He tapped his cigarette into the square glass ashtray; I inhaled all the aromas of the place—the bitter, chocolaty coffee beans he ground in his tiny kitchen, the metallic scent of his cigarette with its platinum haze, the musty wool aroma of the spindly radiator that sat like a punitive, scalding bench, clanking and hissing. I was sitting in the underworld, in that overheated, sealed room, eating a pomegranate seed, astonished that what I'd read in stories was true. I'd been transformed—I'd been allowed to feel beautiful, womanly—although, dashing back across the city to catch the train home, seeing women holding aloft gossamer bags of dry cleaning as if they were domestic angels, and men in suits with briefcases—the entire reasonable world around me—I prayed to the gods: "Change me back!"

But my body had signed a contract. All of our bodies have. Sexuality is woven into us. The crimson sweater, the ruby slippers, and the red vase my parents intended as my inheritance—emblems of the essential life force. Also the field of poppies, for that matter—the opiated fantasy space where the red glow, diffused, dislocated, saturates to the horizon, and you surrender to a delirious dream.

Change me! all those girls call in the *Metamorphoses*, the instant before the salacious god seizes them. Change me!—so that they will not be ravished by what is both savage and sacred. One young woman instantly becomes a laurel tree sealed up in bark, and another becomes a reed; a third is the flower heliotrope, and an entire family of sisters are oaks—members of the vegetable kingdom, all these, although others become rivers, birds, cows—getting their wish fulfilled even as they are, effectively, entombed.

I had wanted to remain static, without knowing it. I had derealized half of my life. I'd been to the underworld but acted as if it were merely a fantasy. Each time I visited, it seemed merely as if I'd had a daydream. I didn't have to tell my husband because there was some crucial way, I felt, that the affair didn't exist. It had nothing to do with my real life, which was with him. There was nothing to tell.

I hoarded what I had, my marriage, but it changed despite my wishes. The instant I embarked on that affair, the old life was gone. I kept waiting for it to return, but it did not. I had performed my own metamorphosis: had become a statue of a girl. I looked real but felt, at a thousand points, my own falsity.

What do the ancients teach about retrieving what's precious from the land of the shades? Orpheus goes down to fetch underworld beauty—his wife. She'd stepped on a viper at their wedding party. The great poet husband descends to Hades and pleads for her: "Reweave, I implore, the fate unwound too fast / Of my Eurydice." Even the Furies are moved by the artist's powers, and Eurydice, "limping from her wound / Came slowly forth." The husband is allowed to take his wife back to the world of the living—with one proviso. He mustn't cast a backward glance.

> The track climbed upwards, steep and indistinct,
> Through the hushed silence and the murky gloom;
> And now they neared the edge of the bright world,
> And, fearing lest she faint, longing to look,
> He turned his eyes—and straight she slipped away. . . .
> The double death of his Eurydice
> Stole Orpheus' wits away . . .

He worried that his treasure couldn't withstand the transition to the world of light. And she was lost again. So, in bringing forth the dissociated, recovered part, a kind of faith is necessary—faith that what we are recovering is valid enough to break through to common awareness, to the brightness of day.

One day in autumn, having arrived early at my desk, I glanced out the window and noticed a woman in a pink party dress with an A-line skirt stepping her way home over the blue-gray slates. She was alive! A jolt went through me. For I no longer was. This sensation assailed me several times in the coming weeks. A man in a top hat smoking a cigar as he walked beside a garden wall—singing! A young woman in mirror boots dashing across Fourteenth Street. The moon itself, swelling wide its mother-of-pearl form until it was an absolutely perfect disc that stained the air around it with brightness, then folding back into shadow until only a steel curve gleamed—as if to say, "Time is passing for you, too." I stared up in disbelief. Each fullness of the moon was a month of my own life. It was a calendar up there. *I must make a change.*

If I could not make a direct change I must make what change I could. I needed to develop my strength in the world, so that I would have the courage to be honest. As I've written earlier in these essays, I decided to try to find a good job, a grown-up job, a job with a real paycheck.

Even just putting together my resume was hard. A voice in my ear kept sighing, what's the point? It will never work. The further I progressed toward my goal, the denser became the air of unreality, as if I had to move through a deepening fog of my own incredulity. NYU's Bobst Library had a copy of an old essay I needed for my writing sample. But, when I stood before that checkerboard-paved space, even pushing the turnstile in the entranceway seemed of preposterous difficulty. So heavy. Advancing across that optical-illusion, syncopated floor, big as a ballroom, absorbed an eternity. "It will never work. Why are you wasting your time?" crooned a seductive voice in my ear.

And then, the library shelf was empty just where my volume was supposed to be. I frantically searched the shelves above, below. Then I checked the abandoned piles on the various desks and carrels nearby, and finally methodically searched from the top of the building to the basement. My book was missing although the system said it was not checked out. Still, the Barnes & Noble at Fifty-Seventh Street supposedly had a copy. I sat down for a moment on a black leatherette bench in the lobby. This bench was sewn with buttons the size of grapefruits, as if, if I pressed on one, the rules of the game might change. The roar of the atrium swirled around, a roller-derby hum as of everyone careering, striding leg over leg, each pursuing their own ambitious course. How tired I was. The slog home would be wearying. Go uptown first? Was the essay at Fifty-Seventh Street actually worth it? Wasn't it likely that I'd open the book and begin reading and find it lacking? Why not close my eyes, just for a moment? Outside a blue-gray dusk held, and suddenly my eyes detected, in an upper portion of the towering glass wall that rose and rose for six stories—a flicker. A flutter was sweeping through the air, high up.

I stared. A dusting of snow. The delicate, descending flakes seemed to spring out of the very air itself. How beautiful! Tears stung my eyes. I didn't deserve it, this gratuitous beauty. I didn't deserve it but it was given to me anyway. Yes, there is hope for you too, seemed to be inscribed in the sky—my favorite words from a book I'd read a lifetime earlier about curing oneself of acne. That book had belonged to my sister, Anita, who'd been afflicted with terrible blemishes, and I'd loved that message. "There is hope for you, too!"—the last words in the book. Anita had tried the Stridex alcohol swabs, the orange plastic medicine bottles of tetracycline. I used to gaze at the dermatologist's soulful, dear raccoon eyes on the back jacket. How kind of him, I always felt—to announce this to each last girl and boy who reads the book. I didn't deserve this beautiful life—I'd failed in more ways than I could count—but was allowed it anyway. I pulled myself up to my feet now, eager to stand in the snow, to see it all around, and stepped quickly, effortlessly, across the checkerboard.

Outside, the snow blazed on my cheeks. The air carried a crisp, acrylic scent, as of everything contracting, consolidating. The swirling flakes tumbled more heavily here, in geometric conical patterns my eyes discerned just for an instant, then no, then yes again, perfectly arranged. Everything seemed brisk, quickened. Of course I would go uptown to the bookstore! A blanket of snow already lay on the sidewalk. Around the streetlights, the flakes pelted quickly, and the sky itself was strangely luminous, as if someone had turned on an apricot lamp behind a white sheet. "Thank you," rang through me, to nature itself. Blue tracks formed where I walked, as if I were at a Fred Astaire dance studio and every step was correct.

If I got a good job—who knew what would come next? Wouldn't I be more fearless? And maybe I could get such a job. Friends of mine had. One could take measures. One could have a result. The chill rinsed down into my lungs. My head felt clear. And slowly I found my way.

* * *

A year into the job, my in-laws told me that something was ineffably different about me. I had more authority. I spoke with greater decision. And seemed simply to have more substance. I seemed happier, too—which I was. Now I only rarely pretended to feel what I didn't. People didn't offer me unsolicited advice, as people often used to—for I had been soliciting it, unawares. I was less afraid of being overwhelmed by others' opinions and voices. My own perspective had clarified.

And, without planning it, I began to let my husband know what I needed, what I wanted. The new job placed pressures on me, and if I were going to get any of my own writing done, I couldn't pretend—to myself as well as him—that my time and energy were unlimited. I felt less beholden; I experienced my desires as more legitimate. My husband and I demanded more of one another—really demanded it. My old conscious and unconscious fraudulence, what I'd thought of for years as my being nice, had leached the excitement and risk out of our marriage. All those white lies I'd fed us—tiny pots of arsenic. At last I surrendered the ersatz world in which I'd lived. I'd acted as if it didn't matter if I left a life-size dummy of myself in my place—as if my husband couldn't tell, and also as if the fraudulence didn't matter to me to me either so long as I had my secret internal real life to return to on the page.

"You are sacrificing your integrity," a friend of mine had told me sagely during the time when I told lies.

"My integrity!" I'd scoffed. "What did that ever get me?"

"That's because you let yourself off too easy," he'd said, and he was right. Now I found a novel strength in integrity; it felt like being connected to one's native ground. This trait that I'd formerly thought was specious, redolent of a certain sanctimony, and a privilege of those who could afford it—now I discovered to be orienting.

And now my response to an argument with my husband was strange—I greeted each with a kind of reckless joy. I'd say what I meant. Who knew what would come next? We were alive! Once he flung his house keys across the living room and I simply stared, one eyebrow raised. But then I had to go teach. In the past I would have phoned him as soon as I could and apologized, abject. Now I didn't want to apologize too soon. There was something interesting and even pleasurable in the emotional distance of this anger. Before, we were both merged and dissociated; we took one another for granted and hoarded our secrets. I walked home slowly after teaching that afternoon, dragging my feet, eyes charmed by the twinkling detritus that scrolled alongside the pavement under the shrubbery—drinking-straw wrappers, the silver paper from some chocolates, leaf mold, the earth's own graphite glitter, the beauty in the covert places.

I was almost sad when the anger was over and resolved, that evening. My husband had acquainted me with something new in him, something dangerous and alive and to be respected. I almost wanted the scary fight to go on because I liked hearing and also saying the alive, scary things we withheld from one another. I was also now able to register what he pointed out about my limitations—especially about the way I tried to control him, and the way I let my negativity infiltrate. "You're as bad as your father!" he'd mutter in a swift sotto voce. My father is a notorious worrier, a notorious pointer-outer of how things might fail. I laughed. He was right. I'd let my drastically constricted sense of possibilities crimp our life.

When the phase of many arguments ended, it left us altered. And in fact it never quite ended—each of us spoke up more now. I no longer envied others. I had left behind the days when I felt others were alive and I was not.

Once, on a trip, we went parasailing. This involved running right off the side of a mountain—to either plunge or be carried aloft on ballooning parachute-silk wings. The moment when your heels leave the hard ground and are racing in air was surprisingly unterrifying—in fact, it was thrilling, instantly. Up one went, carried! You could feel the air supporting you. Quiet overtook all. My husband and I rode over the countryside, each hooked to a separate guide, catching thermals and being hauled aloft, then gradually settling down in the air. And there remained that astonishing silence—imagine an airplane with no hum, a hot-air balloon with no gas roar. From our Oz we surveyed treetops and lush fields, and an almost endless blue lake, occupying a fairy tale that had become true.

Afterwards, in the outfitter's office, Paul's guide showed us an image of Paul parasailing. There he was, smiling, with the entire enormous beautiful landscape of emerald green hillside and patchwork valley swerving beneath him. How enormously dear to look at! I loved him and I loved seeing it. It made me crazy happy.

"Let's see yours," Paul said.

I shook my head and explained that there was no footage of me.

"But I asked your guide to film it," he said, momentarily not understanding.

"And I told him not to. He put the camera away." I'd assumed the recording would be costly (although it was not) and unimportant; I didn't need to memorialize the experience of myself parasailing.

"He put it away?"

"Yes." I shrugged, and got up to leave the office.

"Wait. You know how much you enjoyed seeing the footage of me?"

I nodded. I'd really loved it.

Paul looked angry. "Well, you denied me that pleasure. I would have taken as great a pleasure in seeing you. But now I can't."

I glanced down, stricken. Oh. This hadn't occurred to me. And I understood, for the first time in a long time, that my husband really loved me. I apologized, and told myself: remember this. I wasn't just someone to keep him company. He wanted me, in particular.

So our speaking up and making up continued—the interruption of the hypnosis that wants to continue itself. I can hardly say what a surprise it is to have been married for over two decades to someone you are just beginning to discover.

And, finally, I arrived at an answer to that question I'd carried with me so long—why does the trance state engulf so many of us? We do not want to disturb the world. And we worry that what we have within us, the boon from our adventure, is actually not so important. After all, how could one missing element in our lives be so crucial that it's worth risking everything? But, of course, what's missing becomes of disproportionate importance as long as we lack it. Once integrated into our lives, it is simply another, if magnificent, aspect.

The ancestors in the underworld exhort: I know what life is now that I've lost it. Don't join me in a shade-filled insubstantiality until you must. Cling to life, it goes so fast! Why worship appearances? Do you think you can pretend even to yourself?

The title *Surrendering Oz* started out referring to the subliminal training that girls receive to surrender the world beyond home but it came to mean, for me, surrendering the fantasy spaces that keep us from our power, that convince us that it's better to daydream than to act. And, after all, what a relief it is to quit the life of pretense.

Don't live a shadow life full of delusion, urge the ancestors. Their voices ring in my ears. Shining ahead is the edge of the bright world. Dare we trust that we have a right to bring to the surface what had been buried—the flawed girl with the bitten, wounded foot, the locket image that had been scissored out? Dare we introduce the missing element? An answer resounds from the old masters: Don't doubt, and what you hoped for may be granted. New life. It can follow you only if you continue on. The glowing surface of consciousness shines ahead.

ACKNOWLEDGEMENTS

Even a slender book has many friends. I am grateful to the Institute for the Advancement of the Arts at the University of North Texas for granting the resources that allowed me to develop this manuscript. Many thanks, as well, to Alexandra Enders, Rachel Basch, Yona Zeldis McDonough and Anne Burt for providing astute, useful responses to an early draft of this work. Ann McCutchan, Marina Budhos, Daniel Asa Rose, and Sasha Troyan offered guidance on individual essays. Gary Glickman supported the Oz journey from the outset; Sal Randolph and Priscilla Sneff were grand companions throughout. Bonnie Lovell provided astute copyediting. My greatest gratitude goes to my husband, Paul, for helping me find my way as a writer and as a person.

Books from Etruscan Press

Zarathustra Must Die | Dorian Alexander
The Disappearance of Seth | Kazim Ali
Drift Ice | Jennifer Atkinson
Crow Man | Tom Bailey
Coronology | Claire Bateman
What We Ask of Flesh | Remica L. Bingham
The Greatest Jewish-American Lover in Hungarian History | Michael Blumenthal
No Hurry | Michael Blumenthal
Choir of the Wells | Bruce Bond
Cinder | Bruce Bond
Peal | Bruce Bond
Toucans in the Arctic | Scott Coffel
Body of a Dancer | Renée E. D'Aoust
Scything Grace | Sean Thomas Dougherty
Nahoonkara | Peter Grandbois
The Confessions of Doc Williams & Other Poems | William Heyen
The Football Corporations | William Heyen
A Poetics of Hiroshima | William Heyen
Shoah Train | William Heyen
September 11, 2001: American Writers Respond | Edited by William Heyen
As Easy As Lying | H. L. Hix
As Much As, If Not More Than | H. L. Hix
Chromatic | H. L. Hix
First Fire, Then Birds | H. L. Hix
God Bless | H. L. Hix
Incident Light | H. L. Hix
Legible Heavens | H. L. Hix
Lines of Inquiry | H. L. Hix
Shadows of Houses | H. L. Hix
Wild and Whirling Words: A Poetic Conversation | Moderated by H. L. Hix
Art Into Life | Frederick R. Karl
Free Concert: New and Selected Poems | Milton Kessler
Parallel Lives | Michael Lind

Etruscan Press Is Proud of Support Received From

Wilkes University

Youngstown State University

The Raymond John Wean Foundation

The Ohio Arts Council

The Stephen & Jeryl Oristaglio Foundation

The Nathalie & James Andrews Foundation

The National Endowment for the Arts

The Ruth H. Beecher Foundation

The Bates-Manzano Fund

The New Mexico Community Foundation

Drs. Barbara Brothers & Gratia Murphy Fund

The Rayen Foundation

The Pella Corporation

Founded in 2001 with a generous grant from the Oristaglio Foundation, Etruscan Press is a nonprofit cooperative of poets and writers working to produce and promote books that nurture the dialogue among genres, achieve a distinctive voice, and reshape the literary and cultural histories of which we are a part.

etruscan press
www.etruscanpress.org

Etruscan Press books may be ordered from

Consortium Book Sales and Distribution
800.283.3572
www.cbsd.com

Small Press Distribution
800.869.7553
www.spdbooks.org

Etruscan Press is a 501(c)(3) nonprofit organization.
Contributions to Etruscan Press are tax deductible
as allowed under applicable law.
For more information, a prospectus,
or to order one of our titles,
contact us at books@etruscanpress.org.

CPSIA information can be obtained at www.ICGtesting.com
Printed in the USA
BVOW04s1944150315

391711BV00002B/44/P